STUDY GUIDES
WITH DAILY DEVOTIONS

WHO
DO YOU
THINK
YOU ARE?

MARK DRISCOLL

ACKNOWLEDGMENTS

I'm honored to serve as founding, preaching, and vision pastor of Mars Hill Church. This material was a collaborative effort between many different leaders and myself across many of the Mars Hill churches. I'd like to personally thank all who participated for their love for the Lord Jesus, their heart for His people, and their service to Mars Hill.

I believe this study guide is set apart from similar study materials because it was developed within an actual church community. I've seen firsthand the transforming power of Jesus in the lives of the very people who helped develop its content.

Thank you, Mars Hill Church. I am humbled and honored to serve King Jesus with you. For his glory, and our joy.

—Mark Driscoll

"[The] world's fundamental problem is that we don't understand who we truly are—children of God made in his image—and define ourselves by any number of things other than Jesus. Only by knowing our false identity apart from Christ in relation to our true identity in him can we rightly deal with and overcome the issues in our lives."

CONTENTS

INTRODUCTION

Who do you think you are?

How you answer that question has far-reaching, belief-revealing, life-shaping, and identity-forming implications. Your answer is the one thing that affects everything as your identity writes your testimony and determines your destiny. Tragically, few people—even few Bible-believing, Jesus-loving Christians—rightly answer that question.

People simply don't know who they are. The result is, they go looking to people or things to find their significance. When that happens our idolatry becomes our identity which leads to our misery.

The big idea of this study guide—your identity in Christ—is perhaps more timely than ever. Consider the added complexity brought by technology and the ever growing myriad of social media outlets. On the surface, these sites are all helpful for connecting people so they can get to know one another. But, the truth is we don't know who we are and so we are continually seeking to create an identity, present it to the world, make adjustments according to praise and criticism we receive, and lose sight of who we truly are. We don't know who we are, we don't know who our "friends" are, and they don't know who we are.

You aren't what's been done to you but what Jesus has done for you. You aren't what you do but what Jesus has done. What you do, or even who you portray yourself to be doesn't determine who you are. Rather, who you are in Christ determines what you do. These are fundamental truths that we'll explore in depth throughout this study guide.

DAILY DEVOTIONS

The Daily Devotions are a tool intended for families to help facilitate your time together in the Word of God.

Every day there is a new topic to discuss with lessons that will prepare everyone for the designated passaged from the Bible. There are also a series of questions, illustrations, or exercises to help you dig deeper with life application and a suggested prayer.

Every family is different so don't feel bound by the format. Discuss the content in ways that your family relates to. Also, don't stress if you miss a night or get off track with your conversation. This is something that will inevitably happen, (especially with little kids!) so just plan for it and just pick-up where you left off.

Finally, these devotions are not a to-do-list to mark off. The goal is to help you create a home environment where your family regularly opens the Bible together and grows in love for Jesus, one another, your church, and the people in your life.

Enjoy your time together. Have some fun, enjoy some laughs, and build new memories together as you discover what it means as a family to find your identity in Christ.

HOW TO USE THE DAILY DEVOTIONS

The following devotions are offered with the hope of helping you and your children grow in relationship with one another and with Christ as you discover who you are in Him. Treat them as a guide to your family's devotional time together.

Every day you and your family are provided with a new topic to discuss. The lesson will prepare you for the designated Bible passage that you will read. Then, a series of questions, illustrations, or exercises will help you dig deeper into the passage and apply its message to your life. Each devotion is capped off with a suggested prayer.

Don't feel bound to follow every step, read every word, discuss each question, or pray every prayer. Follow the Holy Spirit's leading, and allow the conversation to progress as you best see fit at the time.

Also, don't stress if you miss a night or get off track with your conversation. This will inevitably happen, so be prepared to just pick up where you left off.

Finally, these devotions are not designed for you to place on your to-do list and mark off when they're completed. The goal of the daily devotions is to help create an environment in your household where your family regularly opens the Bible and grows in your love for Jesus, one another, your church, and the people in your life.

Enjoy this time together with your family. Have some fun, enjoy some laughs, and build new memories together. Discussing *Who Do You Think You Are?* will help you and your family learn who you are in Christ and experience the joy and freedom of a life founded and sustained in and by Jesus.

SMALL GROUP STUDY

This section of the study guide was designed with small groups in mind. Use the guide to keep notes and journal your answers as you walk through the weekly lessons.

Take some time before you meet to review the introduction and reacquaint yourself with the material in order to prepare for group discussion. Begin each time by watching a short video with reflection questions (this is included in the DVD Based Study or the DVD is sold separately) and / or by reading the scripture reflection. Questions are provided for each week and will help you explore the topics.

The last section describes a particular experience for your small group to participate in together. Most of the experiences will be done together as a group; others can be worked on alone. Look at the experiences ahead of time and set aside time or resources as necessary. The experience times are designed to deepen your understanding of your identity in Jesus and gives insights into growing the intimacy of your group and for reaching out to the community around you.

WOMEN'S MINISTRY STUDY

In recent years, Mars Hill church has developed a great women's ministry by God's grace. During the planning meetings, one thing came through loud and clear: the ladies of our church wanted to learn skills to study the Bible, and they wanted to study together.

When the ministry officially launched, we used a small groups curriculum that had been produced for a series we were going through together as a church. What we discovered was that between Sunday services, and midweek small groups, going through the same material again was redundant at times. This is why the Women's study material was developed with an eye toward complimenting weekly rhythms of Sunday worship and small group meeting times.

HOW TO USE THE WOMEN'S MINISTRY STUDY

This portion of the Study Guide is a bit different in that it is an inductive study going through the book of Ephesians from the Bible.

Following the time of study and exploration, application questions are provided to assist small group leaders as they pursue their participants. Directed and purposeful focus on life application seeks to explore questions like: how does what I've learned change me? How does it change my view of Jesus' redemptive action? How does it change my view of others, my obedience, my repentance, and how does it affect how I serve my church and my community?

THE DEVELOPMENT OF THE WOMEN'S MINISTRY STUDY

It was clear that a women's study should be written for women, by women, in different stages of life. A young college single has much to learn from a newly married woman, just as the young married can glean from the wisdom of a woman that's been married for 40 years. And the authors of this content reflect that mix. Some are singles, young married, married with children of various ages (babies to teens), and even empty nesters. The women who wrote and edited this content are some of my wife Grace's nearest and dearest friends. Some of these women we have known for many years seeing them grow as godly leaders in our church. We are deeply grateful for the hours and hours the team of women invested in the creation of this women's study guide. They did so as volunteers with other life responsibilities while still finishing their degree, working their job, raising their family, and serving in ministry. They did so because they love Jesus, they love local churches, and they love you.

I want to sincerely thank the women for creating a study guide that delivers rigorous theological information in a way that encourages practical life transformation.

WHAT IS AN INDUCTIVE STUDY?

An inductive study approach encourages digging deep into Scripture and employs an in-depth reading technique set in a discussion based setting. An inductive study asks the questions, "What does the Bible say, and what does it mean? What do we observe, and how should we interpret it in light of the whole truth of the Bible?"

This portion of the study guide is a great compliment to the Daily Devotional and Small Group material focused on delving deep into the text in a collaborative environment. As you steep in God's Word and apply it to your daily life, my hope is that you'll increasingly grow to encourage one another, pray for each other, confess sin, repent, and live out your identity in Christ in community.

STUDENT MINISTRY STUDY

The Student Ministry Study has been designed similarly as the Daily Devotions but is geared toward students and student leaders. Use it to take notes and jot down your answers to the questions as you go through the material.

Student leaders can download the *Leaders Guide* for free at pastormark. tv/campaignsThe *Leaders Guide* is designed to help assist you in teaching the material in your group.

Our hope is that, by the grace of God, and the Bible, through the power of the Holy Spirit, this Study Guide will help you to live an empowered Christian life. I'm convinced there is not better way to get these truths deep into our souls than through personal study of God's Word in community with God's people.

DAILY
DEVOTIONS

WEEK 1
I AM _____?

DAY 1

He wanted to be someone different to get the attention of a girl he liked.

Aladdin was a common boy who thought he had no chance to be with Jasmine. But after discovering a magical lamp that contained a genie with the ability to grant him three wishes, Aladdin asked the genie to change him into a prince. If he could be a prince, he figured, then he would have a chance to win Jasmine's heart.

Throughout the story Aladdin struggles with who he is and thinks about telling Jasmine the truth. Eventually he gives up pretending to be a prince and goes back to being who he really is.

To his surprise, he discovers that Jasmine loves him just the way he is, not for who he was trying to be. In the end, Aladdin and Jasmine marry and live happily ever after.

Like Aladdin, we don't have to change who we are in order to win God's heart and be accepted by him. God accepts us in Christ as we are. Even better, he changes us into who he wants us to be.

Who do you think you are? Where do we even start to answer this enormous question? Let's start at the beginning.

Read *Genesis 1:26–27.*

We have been created in the image of God. This means that each and every one of us was made to reflect God to others as a mirror reflects our image. Do you struggle with trying to be someone you're not? Why?

Take a mirror. Have everyone present take a look at the mirror and repeat the following message: "I have been created in the image of God."

Now ask, "What are the first thoughts that come to mind when you look in the mirror? Are they in line with what God says about you?"

Prayer

Thank God for creating you in his image. Specifically ask for his help in accepting his truth about who you are in Christ.

DAY 2

You and I were created as worshippers.

As worshippers, we are divided into two categories: those who worship the Creator and those who worship created things. Because of sin, we're prone to worship anyone and anything other than the God who made everyone and everything. This is what the Bible calls *idolatry*. In our own lives, then, idolatry occurs when we make a created thing a god thing, which is a bad thing.

Rather than worship these created things, God calls us to worship him. This doesn't mean we don't enjoy his creation; we just do so as an act of worship to him for his good gifts—not as an act of worship *of* his good gifts.

Read *Romans 1:21–25.*

How do we become guilty of not honoring or giving thanks to God? *(The answer can be found in verses 22–23.)*

What are some things that you put before God? *(Consider those things to which you devote your time and money.)*

On what do you spend your time and money? What does this say about who or what you worship?

Prayer

Ask God to reveal idols in your life so you can repent for worshipping them and worship Jesus wholeheartedly.

DAY 3

Often, the things we buy show others what we want them to think of us. The examples are endless and include such things as our cars, clothes, games, houses, jewelry, toys, and more.

We tend to view our possessions not for their use but rather for what they say about us. This is why many people think that wearing non-designer clothes, driving beat-up cars, or using anything but the newest gadget somehow devalues them.

The root of this problem is not in the mall and the things we buy. It's in us.

It's not a sin to buy things and even appreciate and enjoy them. But when those things become the source of our identity, we are guilty of idolatry. The things we own are like billboards of our lives. They advertise what we value and what we would like others to think about us. What does your billboard say about you?

Read *Exodus 20:17.*

What does it mean to covet? *(To intensely wish for; to strongly desire what belongs to someone else.)*

Are there particular things that you covet? If so, what do those things say about who you think you are or what you find important?

Prayer

Pray that God will protect you from coveting by giving you a greater love for Jesus (Rom. 13:9).

DAY 4

Life is filled with duties, starting with chores when we are young, then homework in school, job requirements in the workforce, ministry obligations in the church, relational duties in marriage, and parental and grandparental responsibilities in our families. Our duties are endless. Often they are noble, but when they become the source of our identity, they can destroy our souls.

At the end of the day, you are not what you do. Your duties do not define you as a person. You are defined by who you are in Christ.

Read *Ephesians 2:8–10; 4:24.*

By what and through whom are we saved? (By grace through faith in Jesus.)

DAILY DEVOTIONS

Why is salvation considered a gift? (We cannot work for it. It is given to us by God, through Jesus.)

What type of work is prepared for us? Who prepared this work, and why did he prepare it? (Good works are prepared for us, and it is God who has prepared them, so that we may walk in them and be blessed. God's "good works" beat any earthly duty that we could ever worship.

On which duties do you base your identity? Discuss.

Prayer

Jesus defeated on the cross every idol in your life, including those duties that you pay too much attention. Pray that God will help you see your idols and then turn from them in repentance to God. Ask him to help you remember that your identity is who you are in Christ, not what you do.

DAY 5

Did you know that God created us for friendship? It's a good thing to have friends and people in your life. But, like all things, this good thing can become a god thing if our friends become the source of our identity.

Who is your best friend? With what group of people do you spend most of your time? How do you treat those who are not your friends or a part of your group?

It's important for us to be aware of the people with whom we spend our time and how they influence us to treat others. Our friends will either move us closer in our relationship with God or farther away from him.

Read John 12:36–43.

Jesus performed many miracles, but did people believe in him? *(See John 12:37.)*

Why did those in charge choose not to talk about Jesus? *(They desired people's approval more than they did God's.)*

Are your friends a good or bad influence in your life?

Prayer

Jesus is your perfect friend who can satisfy your desires for friendship and acceptance. Pray that God will forgive you for not accepting his friendship and help you live your life in full devotion to him, not to other groups or individuals.

DAY 6

What do you long for? To be popular? To get your driver's license? A new gaming system? What we long for can give us a false hope that tomorrow will be better than today.

To live for what we long for is like being a small boat on the raging sea—we're always being tossed about. If our plans go well, we feel great and hopeful, as if nothing could ever go wrong. When things go bad in our plan, we feel terrible and hopeless, as if nothing is ever going to work out.

Who you are is not based on what you long for. Your identity is based on what Jesus Christ has done for you. Look to him and to what he has already done for you, and find your satisfaction in him.

Read *James 4:13–17.*

What are your plans for the future?

Why does James say about making plans and talking about them? *(See James 4:14.)*

Discuss with a group or your family if there are situations and plans that they are expecting to work out in a certain way. Ask them what they would think and how they would feel if things didn't work out the way they expect.

Prayer

Pray that God will direct your longings in line with his longings for your life.

DAY 7

Have you ever suffered? Of course you have. Haven't we all?

As long as we live, there will be some level of suffering in our lives. We often suffer physically, emotionally, financially, mentally, relationally, and spiritually. If we're not careful, though, our suffering can easily shape what we think about ourselves.

As Christians, our suffering doesn't determine who we are. Rather, it leads us to Jesus, who suffered and died for us.

In Christ, we find grace to withstand our suffering and hope that one day, either in this life or the life to come, our suffering will end.

Read *Romans 5:1–5.*

What are the three reasons we can rejoice in our suffering? *(Suffering produces endurance, endurance produces character, and character produces hope.)*

Discuss with your family how they respond to suffering. How does belonging to Jesus make a difference when you suffer?

Prayer

God gives us grace and hope during the times when we suffer. Ask God for his help in experiencing grace and hope in your suffering.

WEEK 2
I AM IN CHRIST

DAY 1

Who's your hero? Have you read his or her biography? We love stories about heroes who accomplished amazing things, don't we?

In every biography the hero rescues him- or herself—or someone else—from a terrible fate. As we read such tales of heroism, we look for sources of hope and examples of courage, dedication, sacrifice, and triumph. Biographies are great—but testimonies are even better.

Testimonies are very different from biographies. A *testimony* is about Jesus—his life, his accomplishments, and his determination in an individual's life. In a testimony Jesus is the hero who rescues us from the terrible fate of sin, death, hell, and the just wrath of God.

What's your testimony? How has Jesus rescued you?

Read *Revelation 12:10–11.*

What are the two ways the accuser, Satan, is conquered? *(By the blood of the lamb and the word of our testimony.)*

How do you defeat Satan in your life? *(By testifying about the substitutionary sacrifice of Jesus Christ on our behalf for the penalty of our sins.)*

This would be a good time to have each member of the family share a testimony.

Prayer

Thank God for being the hero in your life and rescuing you from Satan, sin, and death.

DAY 2

In most sports, coaches lead teams. For better or worse the coach's decisions affect the whole team. If the coach makes great decisions, your team is likely to win. If he or she makes bad decisions, your team will most likely lose.

Christianity teaches us that there are two teams in life, and we play for either one or the other. According to the Bible, one team has Adam as its coach, while the other team is coached by Jesus.

Apart from faith in Jesus Christ, we are identified with Adam, and share in his sin and defeat. But if you are in Christ, you are considered a part of *his* team. Being in Christ means that you share in his perfection and victory.

Read *Romans 5:1–2, 12.*

Who is identified in Adam? *(According to verse 12, everyone.)*

Who is identified in Christ? *(Those who, through faith, have received what he has done for them.)*

Who is the captain of your life? Adam or Jesus?

Prayer

Pray for your friends and family who aren't on Team Jesus, that they will find new life in him.

DAY 3

A tree can tell you a lot about the Christian life.

A healthy fruit tree will grow and bear fruit. But not just any fruit. A hale and hearty tree will bear fruit that you can pick and enjoy eating.

A diseased tree, on the other hand, is quite different. It's likely that it won't grow any fruit. If it does bear fruit, it will taste disgusting. Unlike a healthy tree, a diseased tree can never grow good fruit.

Just as the fruit we harvest grows based on what the tree is, the fruit we produce in our lives grows based on who we are. Apart from faith that is rooted in Jesus, we are each like a spiritually dead tree that produces yucky fruit, what we call *sin* (see Matthew 7:15–20).

If you are in Christ, then you are a new creation, and over time you will produce good fruit, such as love, joy, peace, patience, kindness, goodness, faithfulness, gentleness, and self-control (Gal. 5:16–24). These are known as the "fruit of the Spirit"? How do we get them?

We abide in Christ.

Oftentimes Christians go to Jesus for forgiveness of sin so they can go to heaven, but they leave the gospel behind when it comes to living daily life. Yet Jesus says we must abide in him (John 15:4). What does that mean? It means that we stay put! That we are fed by him daily, and that we flourish as we remain "in Christ."

Read *John 15:4–5.*

Our good works are not produced by our own efforts, apart from Jesus. They are produced by God's work in you—by abiding. Do you seek God's help in living for him, are you abiding in him, or do you try to do it on your own?

Prayer

Thank God that in Christ you are a new creation. Ask for his graceful empowerment to live for and enjoy him forever.

DAY 4

Who do you look up to? Your parents? An athlete? A musician? A politician? A pastor? A superhero? All of us have someone whom we admire, some individual who inspires us, by his or her life, to be better.

We should also look to examples of Christian men and women who live their lives wholeheartedly devoted to Jesus Christ. The apostle Paul is someone we can definitely look up to.

Paul, who was inspired by God to write most of the New Testament, is a towering figure in world history. He lived in an age when cars, buses, motorboats, and airplanes didn't exist. During his time preaching, it is believed that he walked an average of nearly twenty miles a day to share the good news about Jesus with others—even when they didn't want to hear about it.

Paul didn't have a wife or kids and spent a lot of his time alone. Many times he was abandoned by those he considered friends. Even so, Paul gave his all for Jesus and the church—to the point that he even lost his life.

Though Paul died nearly two thousand years ago, we can learn about his life and find inspiration in living for Jesus by just picking up the books of the Bible that he wrote.

As you learn about the life of Paul, be encouraged and inspired to live wholeheartedly for Jesus. You have just one life to live; live it to glorify God and enjoy him forever.

Read *2 Corinthians 11:23–29.*

What do you think about the type of life Paul lived and the struggles he faced?

Do you find encouragement from Paul's life to give your all for Jesus and the church?

Prayer

Pray for your family to be encouraged by Paul's life and example.

DAY 5

When you think of important cities in the United States of America, what cities come to mind? New York City? Los Angeles? Atlanta? Washington, DC?

Cities are important. They influence what goes on throughout the rest of a country, from business and politics to finance and fashion. Even if we don't live in cities, they still play a big part in our lives.

Paul spent a lot of time in the ancient city of Ephesus. If ancient Rome was like New York City or London, then Ephesus was like Los Angeles or Chicago. It was large, wealthy, and influential. In Bible times, the city became a hub for Christian missions.

Many early church leaders were trained and sent out from Ephesus. The city also served as the headquarters of Jesus' youngest disciple, John, who had a level of authority over the seven leading churches of Asia named in the opening three chapters of Revelation. The presence of Christianity in Ephesus was able to influence the surrounding areas. This is why it's not an overstatement to say that had the gospel of Jesus Christ not taken root in Ephesus and spread from there across the Roman Empire, on the trade routes and beyond, Christianity as we know it may not exist today.

Read *1 Corinthians 16:8–12.*

Why did Paul choose to stay in Ephesus? *(A wide door of effective service in the city was open to him.)*

Paul said that a great and effective door had opened to him in Ephesus. Even though God blessed his efforts, does this mean that Paul had it easy? *(Not at all. Paul mentioned that he many adversaries in the area, some who may have even threatened his life.)*

Where you live is no accident. God himself determined where and even when you would live (see Acts 17:26). This week, begin to pray for your city and how you can influence your local community for Jesus.

Prayer

Thank God for giving Jesus authority in heaven and on earth. Ask for his grace to help you fulfill his mission of making disciples.

DAY 6

It's all about Jesus. Our lives are about what he has done for us, what he's doing in us, and what he will do through us.

As a Christian, you are no longer who you used to be. Therefore, you are not identified by your past failures, accomplishments, or sins. Neither are you identified by the limitations you, your family, your peers, or society places upon you. As a servant of Christ, your identity is not based on what others say *or* what you think and feel about yourself. You are identified by what God has said about you. Who you are *in Christ* defines who you are as a person.

In Christ you are blessed.

In Christ you are chosen to be part of his family.

In Christ your sins are forgiven.

In Christ you have good gifts.

In Christ you can glorify God.

In Christ you have eternal life.

Read *Ephesians 1:1–14.*

Reread the Ephesians passage and find every occurrence of "in Christ" or some variation of it, such as "in Him" or "in the beloved."

Discuss what you learned about your identity in Christ from these verses.

Prayer

Pray Ephesians 1:3–14 out loud.

DAY 7

Butterflies are beautiful creatures. From the design on their wings to all the colors they display, they are spectacular. Before any butterfly can be a magnificent creature, however, it must begin its life as a caterpillar, which is quite ugly.

Caterpillars transform into butterflies through a process called *metamorphosis.* Their old nature passes away, and they turn into a completely new creature. Just as caterpillars are changed into butterflies, we, too, are changed into new creatures through faith "in Christ." We transform from ugly sinners to beautiful saints.

Read *2 Corinthians 5:16–17.*

What does it mean to regard no one "according to the flesh"? *(It means that we don't think of someone from the world's point of view, but rather, from Christ's point of view.)*

What are we "in Christ"? *(We are new creations with new identity rooted in him.)*

What has passed away "in Christ"? *(Our old identity apart from Christ.)*

Prayer

Have everyone in your family memorize 2 Corinthians 5:16–17.

WEEK 3
I AM A SAINT

DAY 1

Ruth is a wonderful woman. She is happily married, has five kids, is a foster parent, and helps children in her community who are in difficult situations. People are often surprised to learn that Ruth was once addicted to drugs and even lost her kids for a time to Child Protective Services.

Today, many consider Ruth a saint. And they're right. Ruth is a saint—but not because of the good things she does.

Ruth is a saint because of what Jesus has done for her. Today, Ruth does good things because of the ultimate good thing Jesus did for her. Like Ruth, each and every single one of us in Christ, regardless of our past sins, is a saint because of what Jesus has done for us.

Read *Ephesians 1:1–2.*

To whom was Paul writing this letter? *(Ephesians was written "to the saints who are in Ephesus.")*

What do you think it means to be a saint? *(Biblically, being a saint is not based on the good work you do, but the work Jesus has done for you in living, dying, and rising from death.)*

How does knowing we're saints change the way we live?

Prayer

Thank God for making you a saint, and pray for the saints in your life.

DAY 2

Johnny Cash is a monument of the music industry. He is considered one of the most influential musicians of the twentieth century and was inducted into the Country Music Hall of Fame, the Rock and Roll Hall of Fame, and the Gospel Music Hall of Fame.

Though he was a successful musician, Cash wrecked his first marriage and even struggled at points in his life with drugs and alcohol. In spite his sins, Johnny Cash was a saint. Why? Because he was in Christ.

When reading the different letters of the New Testament, we tend to either read the greetings at the beginning quickly or just skip over them altogether, as if they're not important. If we treated Paul's greeting in Ephesians this way, we would miss something really important. Paul referred to everyone in the church as "saints . . . in Christ" (1:1).

Though many in the church of Ephesus would have been drunks, gossips, or just downright mean people, Paul didn't choose to identify them that way. He knew that if we're "in Christ Jesus," then we're saints. This is why he chose to greet the church in this way.

Read *Romans 7:13–25.*

Why did Paul not understand his own actions? *(He found that he did the very things he hated, and he didn't always have the power to do what was right.)*

To whom did Paul look for help in not sinning? *(He looked to Jesus Christ to set him free from his prison of sin.)*

In Christ, Paul was a saint. Yet in Christ, Paul struggled with sin and doing what was right. In Christ, Johnny Cash was a saint. And yet, in Christ, Johnny Cash also struggled with sin and doing what was right. What can you learn from their experience? *(In Christ we can still struggle with sin, but Jesus Christ—not "being good"—will deliver us from its punishment and power.)*

Prayer

Thank Jesus Christ that he redeemed you from the penalty and power of sin.

DAY 3

How does one become a saint? Do you have to become a church member? Devote your life to a good cause? Preach to sold-out stadiums? Have a large following? Even though many think this is how you become a saint, that isn't the case at all. The Bible paints for us a completely different picture.

You don't accomplish some wonderful thing or perform a lot of religious service to become a saint. Becoming a saint requires you to be in Christ. It's that simple.

Anyone who is connected to Jesus by faith in his death and resurrection is a saint. God's saints are people just like you and me who simply love Jesus and are changed by him.

Read *John 3:1–8, 16–17.*

How can anyone see the kingdom of God? *(He or she must be born again.)*

How are we born again? *(We believe in Jesus Christ.)*

Prayer

You are a saint in Christ. God, in His grace, chose to love and save you. Take a moment and thank God for giving you new life. Afterwards, think of at least five people in your life that you can pray for to be born again.

DAY 4

God made everything out of nothing. He created the universe, the stars, the earth and everything in it. He even created our first two parents, Adam and Eve. Then, thinking about what he had created, God said that it was "very good" (Gen. 1:31). Unfortunately, things didn't stay that way for long.

Our first parents—in particular, Adam—rebelled against God and did what he was told not to do. Adam's single act of disobedience flung open the door for sin to enter into the world. Sin has now infected and affected everyone and everything.

Thankfully, that isn't the end of the story. Though we may be sinners in this life, that's not all we are. We are the image bearers of God, who are made saints in Christ.

Read *1 John 1:8; 3:9–10.*

How do we deceive ourselves? *(By believing we have no sin.)*

Can someone born again continue in the same sin as before? *(No. Someone who is born of God does not make a practice of sinning. He or she will be convicted of it and led to repent of it.)*

Discuss the difference between having sin and being in sin. *(A saint does sin. But when a Christian sins, he or she is convicted by the Holy Spirit and is led to repent. This is the difference between having sin and being in sin).*

Discuss with your family whether there are sins they struggle with on a regular basis, and pray for one another to find freedom from sin in Jesus.

Prayer

Thank God that he has defeated the power of sin in your life. Ask for his help in having your identity be that of a saint, not a sinner.

DAY 5

Everyone has regrets sometimes. There are many things in our lives that we can look back on and feel sorry that we did or even did not do. The most influential Christian of all time, the apostle Paul, himself felt such remorse. Writing to Timothy, a young pastor, Paul expressed recognition of his sinfulness this way: "Christ Jesus came into the world to save sinners, of whom I am the foremost" (1 Tim. 1:15 ESV).

Christians grow and mature as saints in their relationship with Jesus. As they do, they see sin more clearly and grieve it more deeply. It is good for believers to feel remorse for sin, confess it, repent of it, and believe in Jesus' forgiveness from it.

Read John 16:4–11.

Whom did Jesus send after he ascended to heaven? *(The Helper, who is God the Holy Spirit.)*

What does the Helper do? *(He convicts the world of sin, righteousness, and judgment. He, not our conscience, is the One who convicts us of the sin in our life and leads us to Jesus.)*

Ask your family if there have been times when they felt convicted of sin by the Holy Spirit. How did they respond to his conviction?

Prayer

Ask God to help everyone see their sin rightly and respond by confessing, repenting, and turning to Jesus for forgiveness.

DAY 6

As a saint, you will be tempted to sin. But temptation and sin aren't the same.

To be tempted is not a sin. Rather, temptation is an *invitation* to sin. As a saint, you'll be tempted to sin. When—not if—you are tempted, you are presented with an opportunity to either disobey God or worship God. Whether or not you sin all depends on how you respond.

When you are tempted to sin, remember that you're a saint. Knowing your identity in Christ is the key to victory over sin. Jesus modeled this truth for us.

Jesus himself faced temptations but refused to give in to them by remembering his identity and living out of it in the power of the Holy Spirit. Jesus' example is a powerful model for us today. In Christ we are new creations, empowered by the Holy Spirit to deny sin and to worship God.

Read *1 Corinthians 10:13.*

What does the Bible say about the temptations you face? *(They're not uncommon to mankind.)*

How is God faithful to you when you are tempted? *(God will not let you be tempted beyond your ability but will provide for you a way of escape.)*

Discuss times when you have been tempted to sin. What was your response?

Prayer

Pray for forgiveness, if anyone in your family has succumbed to temptation. Ask God to give you strength to endure temptation and to help you see the door of escape when tempted.

DAY 7

"The Tortoise and the Hare" is a famous story about a race. The hare was the fastest creature around, and he knew it. He also let everyone else know it.

Tired of hearing the hare talk about how fast he was, the slow old tortoise eventually challenged him to race.

As soon as the race began, the hare took a commanding lead. Soon, though, he decided to take a nap, since the tortoise was nowhere to be found. But after waking from his nap, he discovered that the tortoise had slowly walked to victory!

The hare's biggest challenge in the race wasn't the speed of the tortoise— it was his own pride. Pride is your enemy, too, but humility is your ally.

Pride tempts us to compare ourselves with others; humility points us to our sinless Savior. Pride covets the success of others; humility celebrates it. Pride is about me; humility is about Jesus and others. Pride is about my glory; humility is about God's glory. Pride causes separation from God; humility causes dependence on God. Pride leads to arrogance; humility leads to confidence. Pride causes me to do things in my own strength; humility compels me to do things in God's strength.

Read *1 Peter 5:5.*

With what are we to clothe ourselves? *(Humility.)*

Whom does God oppose and to whom does he give grace? *(God opposes the proud and gives grace to the humble.)*

Grab a blanket or some item of clothing to represent humility, and another to represent pride. Have two different family members wear the items. Then act out a scene in which they need help. For the person wearing the item representing pride, instead of helping him, act out what it means to oppose him. For the one wearing the item representing humility, act out what it means to give grace.

Prayer

Thank Jesus for modeling humility and serving you in humility by living a perfect life and dying for your sins. Pray that God will clothe your family with humility so each of you will repent of any pride in your life.

WEEK 4
I AM BLESSED

DAY 1

What makes God love us? Is it when we do good things for him? Some people think so. We can easily believe that if we pray, read the Bible, give a lot of money to the church, or live a good life, we'll make God love us and he will be good to us.

Thankfully, this isn't true. You don't have to do good things for God to love you and bless you. He has already blessed you in Christ.

God loves us even when we're sinners. In his love he saves us through Jesus and makes us new people in Christ. We must simply believe it and accept his gift of salvation. That's faith.

Read *Ephesians 1:3.*

With what have we been blessed? *(Every spiritual blessing. These spiritual blessings are from "the heavenly places," and they include our salvation.)*

How are we to respond to God as a result of being blessed with every spiritual blessing? *(God is to be blessed. This means we are to speak well of him by praising him.)*

We are to praise God for the spiritual blessings he gives us. Discuss how this is like thanking someone who has given us a great gift or done something nice for us.

Prayer

Have each family member thank God for his/her blessings in Christ.

DAY 2

If you could have one wish granted, what would it be? Would you wish for money? Power? Love?

After thinking about what you'd wish for, consider this: God has already given us himself.

In this life, God may not give you health, money, a lot of toys, or an easy life, but he has given you the gift of himself in Jesus.

If you're in Christ, then you're blessed by and welcomed into an eternal friendship with God the Father, God the Son, and God the Holy Spirit. Even if you may not appreciate the gift of God himself today, there is no amount of money or power that can compare to God's gift of himself in Jesus.

Read John 17:3.

What is eternal life? *(Eternal life cannot be reduced to a "Get Out of Hell Free" card. Eternal life is knowing the only true God, and Jesus Christ, whom he sent.)*

What do you think it means to "know" God? *(To know God is to know about him and to experience him in a personal, intimate relationship.)*

Think of someone in your life whom you love or consider a great friend. What if that person moved away, closed down her Facebook account, and you no longer heard from her? How would you feel? Would you rather see her and hang out, or get a present from her? Think about your answer, and then think about how you relate to God.

Prayer

Thank God for giving you the gift of himself in Jesus. Ask God for help in not overlooking the blessings you already have in him.

DAY 3

Whom do you think of as "holy"? A priest? A preacher? Someone who does a lot of good work?

Those people may be holy, but did you know that if you're in Christ, God considers you holy as well? Because of Jesus' work on the cross for us, we are "holy and without blame" before God. Jesus exchanged our sin for his holiness, and God now sees us as he sees Jesus, righteous and holy.

Jesus takes our sin and replaces it with his righteousness. Not only that, Jesus also gives us new desires to live a godly life and the strength to do so by the Holy Spirit. That doesn't mean we live without sin. But it does mean that we grow and better reflect the holiness of Jesus Christ each day.

In Christ we are considered holy by God and given the desire and ability to live holy lives devoted to him.

Read *Ephesians 1:4.*

Did God choose us, or did we choose him? *(God chose us.)*

Why did God choose us? *(God wanted us to be holy and blameless before him.)*

In what ways has God changed you and made you more holy because of Jesus' blessing?

How is God leading you to a life of greater holiness to reflect Jesus more?

Prayer

Take two chairs. Place them several feet apart. Have one family member sit on one chair. This chair represents the person's trust in his or her good deeds for salvation. Now have him or her switch to the other chair. This chair represents a trust in Jesus Christ for salvation. Ask: "Is it possible to sit in two chair at once?" *(It's impossible to sit in both chairs at the same time. Similarly, it is impossible to trust in good works and Christ at the same time. We must rely on one or the other. This is what it means to personally trust in Jesus. Faith in Christ and reliance on our good works are mutually exclusive.)*

DAY 4

How would you feel if you found out that Jesus chose you to be his friend before you were even born? Good news: if you're in Christ, he did. The Bible calls this *predestination.*

To be predestined means that God chose you to receive his love, enjoy his grace, and be his friend forever, even before time began. What an amazing truth!

Predestination brings up a lot of hard questions that people have wrestled with for hundreds of years. Unfortunately, these hard questions are argued about more than this great truth is celebrated. Before time began, God made a plan to love and save his people! That is great news!

God's blessing of predestination brings amazing comfort to the lives of his people. Even though we will go through difficult times, we can rest assured that God is good and has good plans for us.

If you're a Christian, then you're on God's predestined path to a relationship with him. You have been preordained to be loved by God and to be known by him. God has chosen to know you, love you, seek you, forgive you, embrace you, and befriend you.

Read *Ephesians 1:4–6.*

When did God choose us? *(Before the foundation of the world.)*

What did God do for us "in love"? *(He predestined us to be adopted as his children through Jesus Christ, according to his purpose.)*

Why did God choose and predestine us? *(To bring praise to his glorious grace.)*

Prayer

Praise God for the blessing of predestination.

DAY 5

Steve and Jan were nearing their destination. Their travels began in the Pacific Northwest in Seattle, Washington, and they were en route to China. This day marked the end of a year-and-a-half-long process for them. They were finally adopting their son—a young boy named Lu Hui.

As an adopted son, Lu Hui is a part of Steve and Jan's family. He enjoys all the benefits of a natural-born son, including the amazing love his parents share with him.

Just as Lu Hui was adopted into Steve and Jan's family, we are adopted into God's family, in Christ. And just as Lu Hui experiences all the benefits of being a son, we, too, experience the benefits of being sons and daughters of God. We are his children, and he is our Father. We have brothers and sisters in Christ from every nation, tribe, and tongue.

Read *Ephesians 1:5.*

What did God predestine us for? *(Adoption.)*

What are we adopted *as*? *(We are adopted as God's children into his family.)*

How is our adoption as God's children made possible? *(Through Jesus Christ.)*

How does it feel to be a part of your family? *(Parents, relate this to being a part of God's family now that he has adopted you into it through Jesus Christ.)*

Prayer

Thank God that you're able to call him Father.

DAY 6

At one time millions of Hebrew people were enslaved to an Egyptian king, called "Pharaoh." When asked by God's servant to let the Hebrew people go, Pharaoh refused to release them.

In response to Pharaoh's stubbornness, God sent a series of judgments upon the nation of Egypt. After the first nine of these judgments, he warned the king that he would next take the life of every firstborn son in every household.

In order to be spared this terrible fate, the Hebrew people were instructed to take lamb's blood and cover their front doorposts with it. God promised that when he saw these painted doorposts, he would pass over their homes and spare the lives of their firstborn sons.

As a result of this judgment against Egypt, the Hebrew people, once enslaved, were freed from their captivity and allowed to live as free worshippers of God.

Just as Pharaoh had enslaved the Hebrew people, apart from faith in Jesus Christ we are enslaved by the power of sin. But in Christ we are freed from its penalty and power in our lives.

Read Ephesians 1:7.

What do we have "in [Jesus]"? *(Redemption.)*

Through what do we have redemption? *(The shed blood of Jesus Christ.)*

This is a good time to discuss what sins you struggle with and are perhaps enslaved to. Encourage your family to recognize that their sin is not their master and that in Christ they are redeemed from its power and control.

Prayer

Thank God that since Jesus died for your sin, you can put your sin to death, walk away from whomever or whatever has enslaved you, and enjoy a new life to worship God freely.

DAY 7

Why does God bless us? So we can make a big deal about how great we are? Or does he bless us so that *he* will be made great?

The entire point of God's blessing is his glory. God blesses us with every spiritual blessing in Christ so that we may enjoy and glorify him forever. This means that our purpose in Christ is to worship God and enjoy him eternally.

Read *Ephesians 1:6, 12, 14.*

According to verse 6, what is the purpose of God's blessings? *(To bring praise for his glorious grace.)*

What is the purpose of God's blessings as found in verses 12 and 14? *(To elicit the praise of his glory.)*

Discuss what it looks like to live a life of purpose in Christ for God's glory and your enjoyment.

Prayer

Pray through Ephesians 1:11–14.

WEEK 5
I AM APPRECIATED

DAY 1

Have you ever felt as though you just wanted to crawl under a rock and hide from everybody? If so, you're not the only one.

Patrick Stump, the former lead singer of Fall Out Boy, a multi-platinum-selling rock band, experienced a great deal of depression when he felt unappreciated by the music industry and his fans.

After the release and failure of his solo album, as well as the negative criticism of Fall Out Boy's latest album, Patrick was left feeling as if he had "received some big cosmic sign that says [he] should disappear."[1] You need to stop for a moment and let his comment sink in.

Patrick Stump, a famous and rich musician, still needed the approval of others. This is true for anyone. No matter how famous or rich we become, we want to be appreciated, and when we're not, the emotions that come with feeling unappreciated can crush us.

We're faced with a choice when we feel this way. Do we believe what the world says about us? Or do we believe what God says about us? What we choose to believe can change the path of our life in big ways.

Read *1 Samuel 18:6–11.*

What is the song the women sang when David returned from battle? *("Saul has struck down his thousands, and David his ten thousands"* [ESV].*)*

How did King Saul respond to this song? *(He grew very angry with David and attempted to take his life because David was mentioned along with him and given credit for defeating more people than he did.)*

Saul's response to feeling unappreciated is an extreme example. How do you feel and respond when you're unappreciated?

Prayer

Ask God for help in finding your appreciation in him and not in how things work out or in what people say.

DAY 2

The next time you're in a lunch line, leaving a game or concert, or getting off the bus, take a moment to observe how people expect you to treat them, and how they treat others. People can be just plain rude. Everyone at one point or another seems to act as if they are more important and that what they're doing has more meaning than anything we do.

No one likes to be treated rudely. Yet we, too, can be rude at times. Have you ever been jealous when someone else won a big award, performed well in a game, or got the latest gadget? How did you act?

We can get frustrated and angry—and even rude—when we're not appreciated for what we do. From work, school, and chores, we can go through the day feeling unappreciated, as if nobody cares. If you've ever felt this way, there's good news for you. God sees everything you do. He knows the sacrifices you make and the work you do. With every good thing you do in Christ, he is appreciative.

Read Ephesians 1:15–16.

What did Paul hear about the people of Ephesus? (He heard about their faith in Jesus and their love toward all the saints.)

Because of what he heard, what did Paul do? (He gave unceasing thanks for them and remembered them in his prayers.)

Talk about what you feel and think when someone is rude toward you. Identity up to three ways you can show appreciation to others.

Prayer

Have your family pray and give thanks for the people in their lives. Have them each identify at least one reason they are thankful for others.

DAY 3

After being delivered by God from Egyptian slavery, the Israelites began traveling toward the land God promised to them. In time, they reached its borders.

But before entering the promised land, the Israelites wanted to send spies to check it out, so they did. Unfortunately, when the spies returned from their trip, most of them provided a bad report. They didn't believe that Israel could go into the land and defeat the people who lived there.

When the people heard this report, they grumbled and wept. They even thought it would be better for them to go back to being slaves in Egypt than to cross over and take the land that God promised. In response to their grumbling, God judged his people. He said that everyone twenty years and older would eventually die in the wilderness and not see the promised land (Numbers 12–13).

When things don't go our way, we are tempted to grumble. To grumble is to complain against God when we're displeased with things.

The Bible is clear that grumbling is a sin (James 5:9). That doesn't mean we have to hide our feelings and just pretend to be happy. When things don't go as expected, we can be honest about our hurt and frustration, but in doing so, we should take it directly to God.

Troubles will come, but by God's grace, we're able to respond in these moments with prayer and trust in Jesus.

Read *Luke 23:32–38.*

If anyone had the right to grumble, it was Jesus. Prior to dying on the cross, he underwent horrendous suffering. How did Jesus respond to those who mistreated him? *(He prayed for them, "Father, forgive them, for they know not what they do.")*

How about you? When frustrated, annoyed, or feeling unappreciated, do you respond with grumbling or praying?

As you think of past examples in your own life, how has grumbling only made the situation worse? What if you exchanged grumbling for prayer?

Prayer

Pray for those whom you have a difficult time appreciating or who have mistreated you.

DAY 4

T-ball can turn into a game more about the individual kids than about the team. If you don't believe it, just watch a game. When a player gets a hit, all the defenders in the area will jump on it instead of allowing the player in the right position to get it. Sometimes they'll even argue over who had the ball first. Why? Because they haven't learned teamwork yet.

Often, in our lives, we engage in the same unhealthy competitiveness—we're just better at hiding it.

Competitiveness is not sinful, but the reason we compete can be. Are you motivated to encourage yourself and other Christians to be more faithful and fruitful for God's glory than ever before? Or do you discourage others from seeking God's best in their lives because you're jealous of their success?

Ungodly competition in the Christian life is when we compete against others. Being in Christ liberates us from ungodly competition and helps us celebrate others and their successes.

Read Ephesians 1:15–16.

Paul set a great example for us. He was someone who could celebrate what God was doing in someone else's life. Did Paul compare the Ephesians' work to his own? (No. Paul didn't compare their work to his own or even mention his many accomplishments.)

What did Paul do as a result of hearing about their faith? (He celebrated the evidence of God's grace in their lives by unceasingly giving thanks.)

Do you celebrate the success of others?

Is God convicting you about anyone with whom you wrongly compete? Repent, and start celebrating what God is doing in his or her life.

Prayer

Pray for others in a way that celebrates their successes.

DAY 5

We get either bitter, or better. It all depends on how you respond to things that don't go the way you think they should.

Children can become bitter and complain when they don't get something they ask for in the store. Teens can do so when they're not allowed to go to a party with their friends. Every one of us is tempted to grumble when things don't work out at school, in sports, with friends, or on our jobs.

We can also get bitter—against both others *and* God—when people don't express appreciation. Some folks even give up, saying things like, "If no one appreciates what I do, why try?" or, "If they're going to be ungrateful, they can do it themselves." Others, while they don't quit, make sure to let everyone know how hard their job is and how much work they're doing, in hopes that someone will tell them how much they're appreciated.

God appreciates everything good that his children do. In Christ you're appreciated. In those moments when you are tempted to become bitter and complain, ask for God's grace to help you respond in a way that expresses thankfulness for his appreciation of you.

Read *Ephesians 1:16.*

How does being appreciated in Christ help you exchange bitterness for thankfulness?

How did Paul model appreciation? *(He knew that in Christ he was appreciated. He could be thankful for God's grace in his life and in the lives of others.)*

Are you bitter against God or someone else? If so, has your bitterness negatively affected your friendship with others and/or your relationship with God? If not, how might such bitterness affect your life?

Prayer

Thank God that you're appreciated in Christ. Ask for his help in being thankful for him and the people in your life.

DAY 6

How do people become great? Do they launch a business and make a lot of money? Do they start a band and play before thousands? Do they make a video that goes viral on YouTube?

Jesus said that our pursuit of greatness is through service, not performance. He modeled this with his own life, laying it down for our forgiveness.

Performance is doing things for other people's approval. Service is doing them for God's approval, knowing that he is watching. Performance enslaves us to the opinions of others, making us unable to say no to anyone. Service frees us to do what God wants, enabling us to say no to others as needed. Performance leads us to become perfectionists, wanting to do everything just right to get praise from others. Service allows us to do even simple tasks and know that we are praised by God for doing so.

Knowing that God appreciates us in Christ allows us to exchange our performance for service.

Read *Mark 9:33–37.*

Did Jesus discipline his disciples for aspiring to greatness? *(No. Jesus redirected their aspirations for greatness.)*

How does someone obtain greatness in the kingdom of heaven? *("If anyone would be first, he must be last of all and servant of all.")*

Do you have tendency to perform or to serve?

Have everyone in your family identity up to three ways they can serve.

Prayer

Pray for a deeper understanding of God's appreciation for you and your family to free you from the pressures of performing and to help you become more satisfied in serving.

DAY 7

Have you ever bragged on Facebook? Did you go on and on about how well you did at school or in a game, or about how much stuff you have? Why do you think you did that? Was it to get the praise of others?

One reason we turn to bragging is because we feel unappreciated. When we feel this way, we can become obsessed about telling others what we've done. Sometimes we do this to the point that we overstate the facts and even lie to impress others with the hope of gaining their appreciation.

Boasting is an ungodly and unhappy path to take. When we boast, we are using people for appreciation. When our appreciation comes from God, however, we can start loving people instead of using them. We can stop boasting and start encouraging others once we believe that God appreciates us.

Read *Ephesians 1:15–23.*

Look through the passage again and discuss how Paul modeled encouragement in his prayers for the Ephesians.

Why would Paul pray for this church to know God better since they already knew God and had been under good Bible teaching? *(Knowing God and knowing about God are different. Our relationship with God needs to be continually nurtured.)*

Is there anyone in your life who appreciates you the way Paul appreciated the church in Ephesus?

By God's grace, commit to being an appreciative person. Have your family identify some ways they can be appreciative people.

Prayer

Pray out loud Ephesians 1:15–23.

WEEK 6
I AM SAVED

DAY 1

Self-improvement messages are nearly everywhere. We see them in magazines, newspapers, and books; on television; in advertisements; and on the Internet. You will find multiple steps to living a better life or to making yourself more attractive, a superior athlete, the smartest student, and even rich.

With constant bombardment of self-improvement messages, we must be careful that we don't reduce our relationship with God through Christ to a series of steps to living the best Christian life possible. When we do this, we belittle God and turn him into someone who helps us achieve what we want out of life.

How do we protect ourselves from adopting selfish methods in our relationship with God? Simple. We live in light of the gospel.

According to A. W. Pink in The Redeemer's Return, the gospel is more than a message about God saving you from the penalty of your sin. It is a message about God saving you from the penalty of your sin, the power of sin, and the presence of sin.

Throughout your life you are brought along by Jesus and lovingly empowered by the Holy Spirit to live for the glory of God and enjoy him forever. So instead of formulating a new series of steps to take, look to Jesus. Preach the gospel to yourself every day as a way of placing your trust for your life in his hands, not your own.

Read *Ephesians 2:1–10.*

How did Paul use the word *saved* in Ephesians 2:5, 8? *(He wrote in the present perfect tense, which indicates an action that was* already *completed at the time of his writing. This means we have* already *been saved from something.)*

From what have we been saved? *(From Ephesians 2:1–3 we see that we've been saved from God's wrath.)*

When talking about being saved, the Bible typically has two ideas in mind: (1) we are in danger and cannot rescue ourselves; and (2) Someone else rescued us.

Be creative and think of ways you and your family could act out a rescue mission in your home that captures these two points.

Prayer

Thank God for his mercy and grace in rescuing you from the penalty of your sins through faith in Jesus Christ.

DAY 2

Plants, animals, and people share two things in common. They live and die.

But did you know that when God originally created everything, including Adam and Eve, death wasn't a part of his creation? Death only came into creation because of sin. Adam and Eve could have lived forever if they hadn't sinned. But they did, and death is a reality for us today.

Christianity teaches that death is the penalty for sin. Because of sin, death entered the world and spread to everyone and everything. Unfortunately, there is nothing we can do to prevent it.

In this life we are also born spiritually dead. Apart from faith in Christ, we are dead to God and separated from him because of our sin. Just as we can't stop physical death, we can't do anything about our spiritual death.

Thankfully, Jesus can.

In Christ we're saved from our sins, the consequence of death, and made alive to God and reunited with him.

Read Ephesians 2:1–5.

How did Paul describe people? *(Apart from Christ, humanity is dead in their trespasses and sins, follows the course of this world, follows Satan, lives in the passions of their flesh, carries out the desires of the body and mind, and are by nature children of wrath.)*

What did God do for us "with Christ"? *(God made us alive together with Jesus Christ.)*

All of us are spiritually like dead men and women before God. We're unable to move toward God unless he moves toward us. We are dependent upon his grace and mercy in revealing Jesus Christ to us. How does this change the way you relate and share the gospel with non-Christians?

Prayer

Thank God that he has raised you from spiritual death to spiritual life so that you may live for him.

DAY 3

Imagine walking for years in the same direction. How far do you think you would travel from home? Pretty far, right?

Spiritually, this is how life is for non-Christians. Every day they walk in the same direction, with their backs toward God and their faces toward sin and selfishness. This is what Paul called walking after "the course of this world." Their travels lead them farther and farther into darkness and death.

As Christians, we are to live lives of daily repentance. This means we are to turn our backs to sin and our faces toward God. We're to walk toward Jesus, day in and day out. In Christ we're saved from walking on this worldly road and turned to walk toward God.

Read Ephesians 2:2.

What course do people walk apart from Christ? *(They follow the course of this world.)*

Whom do people follow apart from Christ? *(The prince of the power of the air: this is another way of referring to Satan.)*

Would you say that you're walking toward Jesus or toward the world?

Prayer

Thank God that by saving you and setting you on a path to follow him, he has delivered you from the need to follow the world and Satan.

DAY 4

If we don't believe in Jesus, then we're on friendly terms with Satan.

You're probably thinking, *I've never worshipped Satan. How could I possibly be his friend?*

We read in the Bible that even if we don't acknowledge Satan as our god, apart from Christ we are subject to his authority.

In Ephesians 2:2 Paul described non-Christians as those who walk "according to the prince of the power of the air"—that is, Satan.

There's no middle ground in Christianity. Jesus says that we are either for him or against him (Matt. 12:30.)

Thankfully Jesus rules above Satan and demons. He has defeated their hold on us through his sinless life, substitutionary death, bodily resurrection, and exaltation to his throne in heaven.

In Christ, we're saved from Satan.

Read *Luke 10:17–20.*

What did Jesus see in Luke 10:17–20? *(He saw Satan fall like lightning from heaven.)*

What do you think it meant for Satan to "fall"? From *what* did he fall? *(Jesus meant that Satan had lost his position in heaven, as well as his place of authority in the lives of people. Through Jesus, Satan's authority has been broken.)*

In 1 Peter 5:8–9 Satan is depicted as a roaring lion looking for someone to devour. We are told to resist him firmly in our faith. Would you say that you resist the devil's influence? Why or why not?

Prayer

Thank God that he has saved you from Satan, and that Satan no longer has authority over your life.

DAY 5

Sandra McCracken, on her album *Live Under Lights and Wires*, tells a story of two young boys who play together near a river. Sadly, the two boys fall into some quicksand. When the rescue workers finally come, they only find the younger brother standing on top of the sand. When the boy is asked where his brother is, he says, "I'm standing on his shoulders." The older brother had sacrificed himself to save his younger brother.

Just like that younger brother, we all are in need of being saved from the quicksand of our sin. Fortunately, Jesus, our older Brother, saves us.

Read *Ephesians 2:1–10.*

Have everyone read through these verses and find ways that Paul contrasted our old nature of sinking in sin with our new nature in Christ.

OLD NATURE	NEW NATURE
Separated from Christ	United with Christ
Dead	Alive
Disobedient	Obedient
Ruled by spiritual evil	Sharing in Jesus' rule over spiritual evil
Objects of God's wrath	Objects of God's affection
Walking in sin	Walking in good works

Prayer

Thank God that you are a new creation in Christ. Consider taking this list, writing it down, and taping it to your mirror to remind you of your new identity in Christ.

DAY 6

There will be a time in your life when you're in trouble and won't be able to save yourself. You'll need the help of someone else.

Each of us is born in trouble. We have a sinful nature from birth. As a result, we've committed sinful acts against God, and we deserve to be punished. There's no way out. No way we can save ourselves. No amount of money, good deeds, or power can save us from God's just wrath and punishment. We need a savior.

Who might that savior be? It's Jesus Christ.

Jesus lived. He suffered. He died. He rose again from the grave. And Jesus lives today as Lord and King. He did all of this for you and me, to pay for the punishment for our sin—a punishment we rightfully deserved. Jesus is the only Savior. Apart from him there is no salvation.

Read *Ephesians 2:4–5, 8–9.*

What did God do to save us through Jesus? *(He was rich in mercy, he loved us, and he extended his grace toward us.)*

Can we earn God's mercy, love, and grace? *(No. They are not the result of works. They are gifts from God.)*

When you sin, how do you seek God's mercy, love, and grace? Have you felt and acted as if you needed to earn them?

Knowing that God's mercy, love, and grace are gifts from him, how does this change the way you go about seeking them?

Prayer

Thank God for revealing your need for salvation. Thank him for pointing you to Jesus Christ, who lived and died for you and your sins.

DAY 7

Once we become Christians, the natural questions are, "Now what? What did God save me for?"

God saved you for good works, and seeing that changes the way we live our lives for him.

Our good works are not done to earn our salvation and God's favor or to make things right with him when we sin. Our desire to do good is not even mustered up by our own willpower. The good deeds we do are empowered and made possible by God's grace for us, in us, and through us. God is at work in you, "both to will and to work for his good pleasure" (Phil. 2:13 ESV).

In Christ you are given the "will," the desire, the aspiration to do good works. In Christ you are even empowered to "work," to choose, to decide to live out the good works that God has prepared for you before you were even born.

Your life matters. You are important to God. He has created and saved you for good works "that [you] should walk in them" (Eph. 2:10). In fulfilling God's plans for your life, look away from yourself, your failures, and your sins. Look instead to Jesus. It is in Christ that you are given the will and ability to live out the life that God has in mind for you.

Read *Ephesians 2:8–10.*

Whose workmanship are we? *(God's.)*

For what have we been "created [saved] in Christ Jesus"? *(For good works.)*

Would you say that the good works you do are in your own power or the power provided in Christ?

Prayer

Thank God that you are his workmanship, and that he has made you and prepared good works for you to do.

WEEK 7
I AM RECONCILED

DAY 1

Think about your best friend. You probably spend most of your free time hanging out, talking, and just having fun with this person.

Imagine getting into an argument with your best friend, and not just any argument, but one that makes you really angry. You delete his number from your contacts. You de-friend him on Facebook. You don't even acknowledge him at school and start spending time with other people instead.

One day your best friend apologizes for starting the argument and asks for your forgiveness. You start spending time together again as if nothing ever happened. Your friendship being restored is what's called *reconciliation*. Your friend has *reconciled* with you.

In a similar way we are reconciled with God through Christ.

We were created to be in relationship with God. The entrance of sin into our hearts through Adam and our own sinful acts caused our relationship with him to be broken. Sin separated us from God.

Thankfully, through Christ our relationship with God is repaired. That means we are no longer his enemies but instead his friends.

Read *Ephesians 2:11–16.*

From today's passage, describe your relationship to God apart from faith in Christ. *(We are separated from Christ, alienated from the commonwealth of Israel, strangers to the covenants of promise, without hope and without God.)*

How close to God are you brought as a result of being in Christ? *(In Christ Jesus we are brought "near" to God.)*

If you're in Christ, is God still mad at you? *(No. Jesus Christ is our peace before God. We are able to draw near to God because of what Jesus has done for us.)*

In Christ you are at peace with God. His judgment and wrath no longer stands against you. How does this change the way you approach him?

Prayer

Thank God that you have been reconciled with him through Jesus Christ.

DAY 2

Have you ever been in a large group but still felt lonely? People tend to hang out with people they know and who are like them. Even in large groups this is true, as we tend to hang out with our friends and avoid strangers.

If you've been in this situation and tried to talk with someone from another group, you probably experienced a feeling that you were breaking through an invisible barrier.

Not only will you experience these invisible walls with people; you'll also see physical walls built to separate people. In other parts of the world, certain people have built high walls, chain-link fences, and concrete structures to separate themselves from others.

One day these invisible and physical walls will be destroyed. Everyone God has reconciled with himself through Jesus Christ will live with one another in peace and harmony.

Read *Galatians 3:23–39.*

Through faith in Christ, we are considered what? *(We are considered children of God. To be a child of God is much more than having a family relationship. Being God's children means we are "heirs" of God and enjoy all the benefits of his family.)*

Is there any difference between people in Christ? *(No. The invisible barriers that separate us are done away with and destroyed. We are all one in Christ Jesus.)*

How should your oneness in Christ change the way you interact with others?

Prayer

Thank God that through faith in Christ you are considered his child, an heir of his promises. Ask for his help in living out your oneness in Christ with others.

DAY 3

Do you ever feel separated and distant from God? Before you were a Christian, did you wonder how you would ever find God? The reason we feel this way is because in our sin, we're spiritually separated from God. Sin is like a spiritual wall between him and us.

Many times we try to break through this spiritual wall by our own efforts, our good works, rituals, and other means. None of these will work. There is only one way to break down the wall of sin that separates us from God.

The gospel of Jesus Christ tears down our spiritual wall. Because of Jesus' work on the cross, we are made right with God through faith in him.

Read *Ephesians 2:11–22.*

A Gentile is a non-Jewish person. If you do not have a Jewish heritage, then you would have been considered a Gentile in Bible times. Read Ephesians 2:11–13 and describe the Gentiles' position apart from Christ. *(Gentiles were separated from Christ, alienated from the commonwealth of Israel, strangers to God's covenants of promise, with no hope and without God.)*

How is our spiritual separation from God bridged? *(In Christ Jesus you have are brought near to God.)*

Your closeness to God is not based on what you do; it's based on what Jesus has done. Does this change the way you engage in spiritual disciplines, such as reading the Bible and praying?

Prayer

Thank Jesus for destroying the wall of hostility between you and God. Examine your life to see if any sin is between you and God, and ask him for forgiveness and reconciliation in Christ.

DAY 4

Preppies. Punks. Jocks. Geeks. These are just some of the groups, or cliques, with whom we identify or in which we place others.

Cliques are groups we look to for friendship, comfort, or even popularity. We believe that if we can make it into or even be accepted by a particular crowd, then life will be perfect. The problem is that cliques are made up of imperfect people. Inevitably, your clique will let you down.

The other problem with cliques is that once we're in one, we tend to look down on those outside of our group. One day, however, this will all change.

In heaven there won't be cliques from which you're excluded. There won't even be separate groups to be a part of. The false hope of cliques will be destroyed. Everyone will be unified in Christ. While we can't live this out perfectly today, we should do our best to live in unity with those who are in Christ, whether they're like us or not.

Read *Revelation 7:9–10.*

How many people will be in heaven? *(Too many to count.)*

Where will all the people in heaven come from? Will they look like you, be from your school, or come from your country? *(Yes and no. Heaven will be made up of people from all over the world.)*

Prayer

Thank God that he has reconciled you and countless others to himself. Ask for his help in seeing his work in your community and around the world among all people.

DAY 5

Racism in America is a problem. You don't have to look long and far to see our need for racial reconciliation. In our communities, schools, and even churches, there's an embedded racial division that separates different races from one another. This is not the way God would have us live our lives.

In heaven, all races will be reconciled together in Christ. We will live in a beautiful harmony with all people, no matter their skin color, language, diet, and culture.

The good news is, we can begin this work of reconciliation today. In Christ we are reconciled, and in him we are to move toward living in such harmony with others.

Read *Galatians 3:28–29.*

Is there to be any division between people? *(No.)*

Why is division between people in the body of Christ done away with? *(Everyone is equal before Jesus Christ. What divides us in Christ is abolished.)*

How would you consider your relationship with people from races different from your own? Is there anything you need to change or repent of?

Prayer

Thank God for creating unity from diversity. Ask the Holy Spirit to help you live out this new reality in Christ.

DAY 6

"I once was lost but now am found." These are the words John Newton penned for "Amazing Grace."

During the earlier years of his life, Newton spent time in the slave trade. At one point, he was even treated as a slave himself.

One day Newton realized that he was lost, without a savior and without hope. But God was gracious and merciful to him. Despite his deep sin, God saved him and gave him a new hope in life. It was a hope not based on how much money or stuff he had, but rather a hope found in Jesus—one that will never fade away.

Like Newton, apart from faith in Christ we have "no hope and [are] without God in the world" (Eph. 2:12).

Apart from Christ you are farther from God than you feared. In Christ you are nearer to God than you hoped. Through faith in the truth about who God is and who he's made you to be, you're reconciled to God in Christ.

Read *2 Corinthians 5:18–21.*

What did God do for us through Jesus? *(He reconciled us to himself through the life, death, and resurrection of Jesus. We are made right with the Father through what Jesus has done.)*

What ministry did God give us? *(The ministry of reconciliation.)*

How do we fulfill this ministry? *(We encourage others to be reconciled to God through Jesus. This basically means that we share the gospel with them.)*

How are you and your family doing with the ministry of reconciliation? Identify up to three people with whom you can connect and share the gospel.

Prayer

Thank God that he has reconciled you to him. Ask for his help and power in fulfilling the ministry of reconciliation (see Acts 1:8).

DAY 7

Our reconciliation with God and others through Christ has tremendous implications regarding how we deal with people.

Paul wrote in Ephesians that "in Christ"(Eph. 1:3) there is a "new man." (Eph. 2:15) This "new man" is an entirely new person who makes up a completely new group. This new group is like a new race of people. They are called *Christians*, and they make up the church of Jesus Christ.

This means that your primary identity is in Christ. It's not based on your skin color, what country you come from, or what group you are involved with. Being in Christ changes the way you relate to others.

In Christ you are able to relate and identify with people from every background imaginable. You can live in greater unity with others because your relationships are based on him.

Read 1 Corinthians 12:12–13.

To what is the body of Christ, the church, compared? *(A human body. We have one body with many different members; so, too, does the church.)*

The body of Christ is made up of people from all walks of life with a host of differences. How is this possible? *(The unity of the body of Christ, the church, is accomplished by everyone in Christ being baptized by the Holy Spirit into the body of Christ. Unity among diversity is accomplished by God the Holy Spirit.)*

Prayer

Thank God that in Christ you have been included in the body of Christ. Ask the Holy Spirit to help you better reflect unity amid diversity.

WEEK 8
I AM AFFLICTED

DAY 1

Being a Christian isn't easy.

If you are a Christian, there will be times in your life that are hard. People will make fun of you, think less of you, or even verbally and physically assault you, just because you're a Christian. As a Christian, you should expect to experience some level of suffering in your life.

We worship a God who came to earth and was afflicted. Jesus experienced a great deal of suffering. He was wrongfully arrested, beaten, verbally assaulted, tortured, and made to carry the very wooden cross to which he would be nailed, to die for you and me.

Not only has Jesus suffered. So, too, have those who have faithfully served him throughout history. Even today thousands of people around the world will die martyrs' deaths for their faith in Jesus Christ.

In spite of the pain and suffering these martyrs endured, they lived for Jesus, because Jesus lives.

Read John 15:18–21.

Did the world love or hate Jesus? *(The world hated Jesus, and because they did, they persecuted him to the point of death.)*

Should we expect the world, in particular non-Christians, to love our beliefs and us? *(No. We are not greater than Jesus and should expect the same hatred he faced as we live our lives for him.)*

Have you ever experienced any negative reactions from others because you identified yourself as a Christian? How did you respond?

Prayer

Thank Jesus that he suffered and died for your sin. Ask for God's grace to help you face affliction in your life for your faith in Jesus.

DAY 2

Sometimes, when we suffer, we are tempted to question whether God is good and even whether he's in control by asking, "Why?"

Some of us do believe God is in control, but we don't believe he is good. We think God is cold, distant, and unable to comfort us.

Others are tempted to believe God is good but that he's not in control. We create an image of God who doesn't *want* suffering in our lives and world, but who is powerless to stop it.

When we question God, we are left without help or comfort because our false image of him distorts who he really is. To question God in this way places us in a seat in which we were not meant to sit: the Judge's chair.

When you're tempted to ask, "Why?" instead, by God's grace, ask, "Who?" *Who* is in control? *Who* is it that loves me? *Who* can I go to for help?

The "who" question does not seek answers from God as much as it seeks God himself. The "who" question seeks to grow in deeper understanding of who God is and even who we are, because when we're suffering, we need more than answers. We need God.

The Bible reveals that God is in control, and he's good. For those in Christ this means that everything in life, including our suffering, either comes from or passes through his hand. Be encouraged at this, for God uses suffering for our good, even if it was intended by the enemy for evil.

Read Genesis 50:20 and Romans 8:28.

When you experience some level of affliction or suffering, do you have a tendency to ask God why?

How could asking the "who" question instead of the "why" question help us in the midst of our suffering? *(The "Who?" question will help us find God himself, not just the answers we want from God.)*

Prayer

Pray Psalm 119:46–50: "I will also speak of your testimonies before kings and shall not be put to shame, for I find my delight in your commandments, which I love. I will lift up my hands toward your commandments, which I love, and I will meditate on your statutes. Remember your word to your servant, in which you have made me hope. This is my comfort in my affliction, that your promise gives me life" (ESV).

DAY 3

When was the last time you were discouraged? Was it when you performed poorly on an exam and got a bad grade? Did you make a mistake in a game that caused your team to lose?

All of us are discouraged at some point. There will be a time in your life that you will be discouraged, in school, sports, hobbies, and even your friendships. When it comes, you'll be tempted to give up and quit caring.

You'll even be discouraged in your pursuit of Jesus. There will be a time when you'll be tempted to quit caring about living for him.

When this happens, you'll feel guilty and ashamed, as if you're the only one who ever felt that way. You're not. Even Jesus Christ was tempted to give up.

Before enduring horrendous pain and suffering, Jesus was discouraged. He was tempted to not go through the agony of the cross. Thankfully Jesus didn't give up. He had you and me in mind. He knew that he had come to save his people from their sins (Matt 1:21).

Even though following Jesus Christ doesn't mean that your life will be easy and pain free, trusting in Jesus, who suffered for you, will empower you to endure any level of suffering you experience.

Jesus didn't give up on you. He endured suffering to the point of losing his life for you. Since Jesus persevered and kept pushing through, in Christ we, too, can persevere and continue our pursuit of Jesus when we suffer.

Read *Ephesians 3:1–13.*

How do Paul's words to the Ephesians take on new meaning when you realize that Paul was most likely lying on a cold floor in the dark with an aching body from repeated beatings in prison?

What do you believe is the secret to avoiding discouragement, bitterness, unbelief, and anger while suffering?

DAILY DEVOTIONS

Prayer

Ask for God's grace to help you and your family to not lose heart in the middle of any suffering or affliction.

DAY 4

There's a lot of bad news on television. From forest fires, to floods, to hurricanes and murder, it seems as if the news stations don't have anything to report but bad news.

After watching the evening news, you might begin to think, *What's the point of all this suffering?* Good question. You may also have wondered why *you* suffer, just because you're a Christian.

The pain we endure as Christians leads us to think more deeply about the suffering of Jesus. He suffered greatly for our sins. Jesus endured such pain for one primary purpose: to glorify God the Father.

If you're in Christ, then you, too, can endure suffering for the glory of God. The next time you go through a period of affliction, don't waste it. Jesus didn't suffer so that you wouldn't. He suffered so that as you suffer, you will become more like him and point more people to him, the suffering servant.

Read Isaiah 53:4–12.

These words written by Isaiah were jotted down several hundred years before Jesus was born. This passage is considered prophetic in that it foretold who the Messiah would be and what he would endure.

What do you learn about Jesus from these verses?

Is there anything in particular that stands out?

Becoming like Jesus in suffering requires first reflecting on his suffering. What does reading through this prophesy, which describes the suffering Jesus would endure for you, make you think and feel?

Prayer

Thank Jesus for enduring suffering and tasting death on your behalf.

DAY 5

A cancer survivor has an amazing ability to speak encouraging words to someone going through the same battle that she once did. Have you ever been encouraged by someone who has gone through the same thing you have? Have *you* ever been the encourager?

When we are afflicted and experience a difficult time, we are given an opportunity to comfort others with the same comfort we have received from God. This is one of the many reasons we experience affliction in our life: to comfort others.

God will take care of you in your time of need, and his comfort for you is intended to be passed on to others. In the words of the apostle Paul, "Bear one another's burdens, and so fulfill the law of Christ" (Gal. 6:2).

Read *2 Corinthians 1:3–7.*

Why does God comfort us in our affliction? *(So we can comfort others who suffer affliction, with the same comfort we received from God.)*

Is there anyone in your life who is experiencing an affliction similar to one you have experienced? How can you comfort that person?

Prayer

Thank God for the grace you've experienced in suffering. Ask for his help in leading you to comfort those experiencing similar affliction.

DAY 6

Is the purpose of your life to avoid suffering? You'll be hard-pressed to hear messages that encourage you to do what's right, even if you have to suffer as a result.

Some Christians have a tendency to avoid suffering at all costs, as if Jesus died to provide them a life of comfort. Other Christians just ignore their suffering and how hard things are by flippantly saying, "I'm okay. God is in control." Both of these responses are wrong. If we live our lives like this, we will miss out on the three features of affliction that help us grow as Christians.

First, when we are afflicted, we gain a deeper understanding of how humble and gracious God is to serve us as our Suffering Servant, Jesus Christ.

Second, affliction helps us learn to better love and appreciate those who serve us. We discover how deep someone else's love for us is when we are hurting, needy, and inconvenient.

Third, as Jesus and others serve us in our affliction, we learn new ways to serve those who suffer.

Suffering is not to be avoided or ignored. Even though you may feel as if your life is going in a downward spiral, it's not. Suffering is one of God's ways for you to grow more into the image and likeness of Jesus.

Read *2 Corinthians 1:8–11.*

Why did Paul and his companions experience such great affliction that they despaired of life? *(Their affliction placed them in a position that required them to rely on God.)*

What did God do for Paul and his companions during their affliction? *(He delivered them.)*

Can we trust God to deliver us from our afflictions? *(Yes. We can set our hope on God that he will deliver us.)*

Prayer

Pray this prayer from Romans 15:13: "May the God of hope fill you will all joy and peace in believing, so that by the power of the Holy Spirit you may abound in hope" (ESV).

DAY 7

How would you like to be perfect? Be prepared to suffer. As the Scriptures teach, we become *perfected* through suffering (Heb. 2:10).

For Jesus to have become perfected doesn't mean he wasn't God or that he had sin in his life. It means that through suffering Jesus was able to fully identify and sympathize with us in our suffering.

In the same way, we are able to identity and sympathize with others who experience the same things we do. The suffering we experience gives us an ability to speak into their lives. In a sense we gain a level of credibility with others. We're able to speak about difficult subjects in a way that helps bring healing and life to those who go through the same struggles that we have.

Don't waste your suffering. Allow God to use what you experience to speak into the lives of others. Point them to an eternal source of comfort in Jesus. He is the one who suffered and died for them and is able to fully identity and sympathize with them.

Read *Hebrews 2:10.*

What did Jesus become as a result of the suffering he endured? *(He became perfected. This is another way of saying Jesus was matured through the suffering he endured.)*

How does Jesus' suffering encourage you to approach him with your own suffering?

Prayer

Thank Jesus that he is able to sympathize with you in your suffering.

WEEK 9
I AM HEARD

DAY 1

If you have a wireless phone, then you have probably dropped a call before. You're in the middle of a conversation and you're carrying on about your day, only to find out that no one is on the other end, listening. At this point you may have repeated the question asked by Verizon's test man: "Can you hear me now?"

Thankfully, God never loses reception.

God cares about you deeply. He will always have the time to listen to what you have to say—even if it's something silly or small. If you're in Christ, then God hears you. Always.

This explains why the Bible tells us to pray "without ceasing"—that is, to pray anytime, about anything, anywhere.

In Christ, God is your Father, and you should talk to him regularly, not because you have to, but because you get to.

Read *1 Thessalonians 5:17.*

How are we to pray? *(Without ceasing.)*

What does it mean to pray without ceasing? *(It means to pray anytime, anywhere, about anything.)*

You can illustrate this with you children by using a phone or television cord. Show them that just as the phone or TV is always connected to the wall, we are continually connected with God.

Prayer

Thank God that you are able to pray anytime, anywhere, and about anything.

DAY 2

Centuries ago, if you found yourself in the presence of a king or queen, you were required to kneel. For the rulers, this was a sign of recognizing their authority. For the citizens of their territory, it was a way of expressing submission to their rule.

Today, people rarely kneel for anyone, as it's a sign of submission, honor, and humility. When you kneel, you are giving someone great authority and dignity without even saying a word.

Kneeling before God is a way for us to express our submission, honor, and need for him. We don't need to kneel before God for him to hear us, but we should kneel before God because he deserves it.

By kneeling, with our hands raised in prayer, we appear like soldiers in surrender and like children reaching out to their father, which in many ways is what prayer is all about—surrendering to your Father.

Read *Ephesians 3:14.*

What did Paul do in response to God's work through the gospel in Ephesians 3:1–13? *(He bowed his knees before the Father.)*

How would you consider your posture toward God? Is it one of humility, or pride?

Prayer

Tonight, it would be appropriate for everyone to kneel together in prayer. Thank God for who he is and what he has done and is doing in and through your lives.

DAY 3

How do you think of God? Is he like a mean, old man who is cold, distant, and harsh? Or do you see God as a loving father who is warm, close, and affectionate? How we view God is crucial to the way we approach him in prayer.

If we see him as an old, mean man, then we will rarely—if ever—approach him in prayer. If we understand that God is Dad, then we will naturally speak to him anytime about anything because we know we're loved, cared for, and safe with him.

Jesus called God "Father." He taught us to call God our Father as well. So, talk to your Dad. He's listening.

Read *Ephesians 3:14–15.*

What does Ephesians 3:15 say about God the Father? *(From him every family in heaven and on earth is named.)*

What do you think this means? *(It means that God is the Father of all things, which is another way of saying that he is in control over all of creation.)*

Do you have a difficult time accepting that God is your Father? Why or why not?

Prayer

Thank God that he is your heavenly Father. Thank him for the love and care he expresses for you.

DAY 4

Everyone is needy. Whether you're rich or poor, strong or weak, you need air to breathe, water to drink, and food to eat. You need shelter to protect you from the weather, and clothes to cover your body. You are in need of safety, love, family, and friends.

But God is not dependent upon anything. He is completely and wholly satisfied in himself. While God is in need of nothing, everything and everyone is in need of him. It is said, "All things were created through him and for him. And he is before all things, and in him all things hold together" (Col. 1:16–17 ESV).

Thankfully, God doesn't avoid us because we're needy. He is a good Father and a generous giver who welcomes us to ask for anything. Your Father in heaven knows you have needs, and he will perfectly meet them. So don't be afraid to approach him with your requests.

Read *Ephesians 3:16–17.*

Who provides us with the power of God? *(The Holy Spirit. He is the means by which God's power is available to those whose faith is in Jesus.)*

Why did Paul pray for the church to be strengthened with power through the Spirit in our inner being? *(So that Christ may dwell in our hearts.)*

What does it mean for Jesus to dwell in our hearts? *(It means that Jesus will make each of our hearts his home and keep working on all the broken, dirty parts of our lives in an ever-improving home project.)*

Prayer

Pray Ephesians 3:16–19, "that according to the riches of his glory he may grant you to be strengthened with power through his Spirit in your inner being, so that Christ may dwell in your hearts through faith—that you, being rooted and grounded in love, may be able to comprehend with all the saints what *is* the width and length and depth and height—to know the love of Christ which passes knowledge; that you may be filled with all the fullness of God."

DAY 5

Jesus loves you. How do you feel when you read that? Do you doubt it because you're suffering? Do you disbelieve it because there's great sin in your life? Do you dismiss it because you're so busy with life that you don't have time to think about it?

If so, then remember the prayer Paul prayed for the church, saying, "I pray that you, being rooted and established in love, may have power, together with all the saints, to grasp how wide and long and high and deep is the love of Christ, and to know this love that surpasses knowledge—that you may be filled to the measure of all the fullness of God" (NIV).

In praying this prayer, Paul didn't doubt that God loves his people, but he did doubt that they truly knew it, really believed it, and were experiencing it. Many Christians today know God loves them, but they know it like someone who takes a driver's education class but never drives a car.

Paul wanted the love of God, like a plant rooted deeply in nourishment and able to flourish, to be a deep root in people's souls. He wanted his readers to know that God's love is wide enough to welcome anyone, long enough to stretch from the beginning to the end of time, deep enough to reach down to the worst of sinners, and high enough to transport us to God's heavenly kingdom.

Read *Ephesians 3:17–19.*

What did Paul pray for the church to be rooted and grounded in? *(Love.)*

What did he pray they would have the strength to do? *(To comprehend, to grasp, the love of Christ.)*

Why would Paul want to pray such a prayer for Christians? *(Because God is love, and the world knows that we are his by the way we love.)*

For illustrations you could have your children make movements to illustrate the breadth, length, height, and depth of Jesus' love. (Think of "Head, Shoulders, Knees and Toes" as an example.)

Prayer

Pray Ephesians 3:17–19: "So that Christ may dwell in your hearts through faith—that you, being rooted and grounded in love, may have strength to comprehend with all the saints what is the breadth and length and height and depth, and to know the love of Christ that surpasses knowledge, that you may be filled with all the fullness of God" (ESV).

DAY 6

Do you believe deep down in your gut that God can do more than you ask or imagine? What do your prayers reveal about your trust in God? Do you pray as big as your Father?

Not only is our all-powerful, crazy-generous God at work; he is "at work within us" (Eph. 3:20 ESV). And God's power working in us gives us hope.

In Ephesians, Paul modeled prayer that expects God to continue working in us by the power of the Holy Spirit. In light of God's power at work in us, we should pray expecting to be heard, if we pray within God's will.

Read *Ephesians 3:20–21.*

What is God able to do? *(Far more than we could ask or think.)*

How is God able to accomplish this? *(By the power at work within us.)*

What do your prayers reveal that God is able to do?

Prayer

Ask God to enlarge your vision of him and show you that he is able to do far more than you could ever think or imagine.

DAY 7

Have you ever listened to someone praying? You can learn a lot about people when you listen to them pray. You learn who or what is on their hearts and minds, what they care about, and where their passion lies.

You can also learn a lot about yourself by listening to how you pray. In prayer, your heart and motives are exposed.

What do your prayers say about you?

Read *Ephesians 3:20–21.*

What is to be given to God, and for how long? *(Glory is to be given to God, and it is to be expressed throughout every generation, forever and ever.)*

What do your prayers reveal about you? What would people learn about you from your prayers?

Prayer

Pray Ephesians 3:20–21, "Now to him who is able to do far more abundantly than all that we ask or think, according to the power at work within us, to him be glory in the church and in Christ Jesus throughout all generations, forever and ever. Amen" (ESV).

WEEK 10
I AM GIFTED

DAY 1

Parents, whenever possible, include your kids in your work. Get them involved around the house as you do chores, or if you can, take them to work with you sometime. You can probably do all the work yourself, but that's not the point. The point is to include your children as a way of spending time with them. In the process they will gain a greater sense of ownership and accomplishment. This time together allows everyone involved to get to know one another better. It is the same with God and us.

God is a Father, and serving him in any area of life is like going to work with your Dad. As Jesus said, "I must be about My Father's business" (Luke 2:49). The majority of Jesus' ministry years were spent as a carpenter, glorifying God and serving people by working with his adoptive father, Joseph. He spent the last three years of his life preaching, teaching, healing, feeding, evangelizing, leading, and more. Today, Jesus is still doing ministry.

You may not be called to full-time ministry on staff at a local church, but if you are in Christ, you are called to the "work of ministry." This ministry work includes loving and serving people on your job and in your family, church, and community, on behalf of Jesus Christ. Jesus' ministry on earth continues through you.

In Christ, the Holy Spirit gives us spiritual gifts, which enable us to do meaningful ministry. In Christ, you are gifted.

Read *1 Corinthians 12:4–11.*

Who provides the variety of gifts, service, and activities that we have in life? *(It is God who gives and empowers the gifts we have in life.)*

According to 1 Corinthians 12:7, why does God give us gifts? *(For the common good of the body of Christ.)*

DAILY DEVOTIONS

What do you consider to be your spiritual gifts? Are you using them the way God intends, for the common good of the body of Christ?

Prayer

Thank God that he has gifted in you in Christ.

DAY 2

Most people have been picked last for a game. When this happens, we feel unwanted. This isn't the case with Jesus and the church. We will never be picked last. Instead, we are all invited by him to help as he builds his church.

You may not realize this, but God has gifted you. You have been given spiritual gifts and even natural talents, such as artistic skill, musical ability, athletic prowess, and more. Both spiritual gifts and natural talents are God-given ways to do the work of the ministry. God gave you these gifts and talents as a way for you to enjoy him as you glorify him and serve the church.

By God's grace, glorify him by using the gifts and talents you have in service in and through the church.

Read 1 Corinthians 12:14–26.

In Christ, does God allow us to say that we are not needed? *(No. Even though we may not consider our gifts and talents "special," God does. We are no less needed or a part of the body of Christ based upon our gifting and talents.)*

Why are we needed? *(God has arranged the body of Christ as he chose so that all its members may care for one another. This is why we are not allowed to excuse ourselves, or others, who are in Christ from serving the church.)*

Does knowing that you have been invited to serve Jesus and his body change your perspective about your role in the church?

Prayer

Thank God that he has given you gifts and talents. Ask for his help in using them to serve him in and through the church.

DAY 3

All of us have abilities and roles. Some people are exceptionally gifted and serve on a big stage for the world to see. Others are more modestly gifted and serve behind the scenes. But in Christ, it doesn't matter how influential our gifts are or how famous we are for our service. All that matters is that we steward well what he's blessed us with.

God has given you natural talents and spiritual gifts. His desire is for you to humbly serve him with what he has given you. We are to be faithful with what we have, not what others have been given.

Instead of comparing your gifts to the level of talent or giftedness in others and worrying that you may not compare, by God's grace be thankful for what he has given you.

Read *Matthew 25:14–30.*

In the parable of the talents, was everyone given the same number of talents? *(No. To one the master gave five, to another he gave two, and to one he gave one.)*

How were these different people held accountable? *(In Matthew 25:20–23 we see that they were each held accountable for how faithful or unfaithful they had been with the little the master had given them.)*

What do we learn about serving God with our talents in the master's words in Matthew 25:27? *(We are to be faithful with what God has given us.)*

Prayer

Thank Jesus that he was faithful with his life. Ask for God's help in empowering you to be faithful to him with your gifts.

DAY 4

For someone to have a spiritual gift does not mean he or she is spiritually mature. There's a huge difference between spiritual giftedness and spiritual maturity. One does not equal the other.

Just because you may have an ability to teach, preach, or even do something miraculous, it doesn't mean you're in Christ.

Sometimes gifted people aren't mature people, which is deceptive to them and dangerous for others. By God's grace we should cultivate not only our gifts but also our maturity. How do we do this? By humbly relying on Jesus and the power of the Holy Spirit.

Read *Matthew 7:21–23.*

Will everyone who identifies him- or herself as a Christian make it to heaven? *(No. Not everyone who says, "Lord, Lord" will enter the kingdom of heaven.)*

Will everyone who prophesies, casts out demons, or does mighty works in the name of Jesus enter the kingdom of heaven? *(No. Your spiritual gifts and good works do not guarantee your entrance into heaven. Jesus does.)*

Your relationship with Christ is not based on what you do for Christ. It's based on what he has done for you. Does this passage change the way you consider your relationship with God or the relationships of others with God?

Prayer

Thank Jesus for dying for your sins to pay the penalty you deserve. Ask God to give you a sensitive conscience to see if you have been looking more to your gifts and good works than to Jesus for your righteousness.

DAY 5

At some point you have probably been required to do something at which you weren't skilled. From playing a different position on a team, to working on a school assignment or helping out around the house, there are countless things we are asked to do that we're not good at.

We must be willing to serve outside of our areas of giftedness and talent, even for the local church. There will be times when the church has a particular need. You may not be the most gifted or talented person to do the job, but God may be calling you to help for a limited time.

The church is like a family. We are brothers and sisters in Christ. As a family, we pitch in to help as needed. So, serve where you're needed, even if it's only for a time. And do so joyfully.

Read *Acts 6:1–7.*

How were the apostles serving the early church? *(Not only were they praying and preaching; they were helping those in need.)*

How did the apostles respond to the growth of the church? *(They appointed others to oversee distribution to the needy.)*

We can learn from the apostles' example. There was a need, and they met it for a period of time. Are there needs at your local church? Are you able to help meet that need for a limited time?

Prayer

Thank God for the example of the apostles. Ask for God's help to allow you to better see and meet the needs of your church.

DAY 6

Have you ever seen a kid refuse to try a new food, only to exclaim after trying it that it's "the best thing ever"?

You'd think we'd outgrow this, but we don't. For instance, some people in the church are adamant that they know their spiritual gifting and won't serve in any other area of the church. In their refusal, they might just be missing out on "the best thing ever."

The best way to discover your gifts and talents is by trial and error. Find a place to serve in a church that interests you, and see how it goes. If it's not a fit, don't be discouraged. Simply try something else until you find your place.

As you discover and use your gifts, God will be glorified and others will be encouraged.

Read 1 Peter 4:10–11.

How are we to use our gifts? *(In service to one another.)*

Why are we to use our gifts? *(So God will be glorified through Jesus Christ.)*

Prayer

Thank God for giving you gifts and talents. Ask him to provide the strength you need to serve him, the church, and others with your gifts.

DAY 7

Spiritual gifts and natural talents are given to us by God to glorify him. Unfortunately, due to the presence of sin in our lives, these abilities can be a source of pride for people. When this happens, we use our giftedness as a way of glorifying ourselves, not God. This isn't how it should be.

Gifts are important. Talents are amazing. But these are not the most important things in the life of a Christian. There is a "more excellent way" to live as a Christian than by simply using our skills (1 Cor. 12:31). It is walking in *love*.

You can be the most gifted person in the world, but if you don't have love, then your gift is worthless in God's sight. Our giftedness should encourage us to humbly seek God and ask that he would give us hearts to love and serve the church.

Read *1 Corinthians 13:1–13.*

If we don't have love, do we have anything? *(No. No gift, giving, or sacrifice will amount to anything if we don't have love.)*

How is love described in 1 Corinthians 13:4–7? *(It is unselfish. How?)*

Which is the greatest: faith, hope, or love? *(Love.)*

Prayer

Thank Jesus that as God he modeled a life of humility and service in sacrificing himself for us. Ask for God's grace to help you humbly serve him and the church with your gifts and talents, in love.

WEEK 11
I AM NEW

DAY 1

Hannah grew up in a Christian home, and her family was heavily involved in the church. But after a fallout with the lead pastor, her parents stopped going to church during her high school years. This changed everything for Hannah.

Hannah's mom and dad wanted her to own her own faith and never encouraged any particular belief. This passiveness on their part left Hannah struggling to find her identity during her teen and college years. It wasn't until her junior year in college that God led Hannah back to church.

During this time Hannah began a long and difficult process discovering who she was. The result of this process of grace in Hannah's life was that she experienced a completely changed outlook on life and a new way of living. She was made new in Christ.

In Christ we are all made new. We discover in him who he has made us to be.

Read *Ephesians 4:24.*

What are we created to be in Christ? *(New creations.)*

After what is our new identity in Christ created? *("After the likeness of God in true righteousness and holiness"* (ESV). *This was Paul's way of saying that God's image in us from the beginning is restored in Christ).*

You can illustrate this with your children by using a dirty coin. We are created in the image of God, and in Christ that image is restored, just as dipping the coin in polish restores an image stamped on a coin.

Prayer

Thank God that you are a new creation in Christ.

DAY 2

Do you desire to become a "new you"? You're not the only one. Countless others know this and are trying to get your money to help you with your transformation.

Nearly every cover of the most popular magazines and books, the topics of the most popular radio and television shows, and the most trafficked blogs and websites are about one thing: becoming a new you.

But no matter how much we change or what we accomplish as a result, our efforts to use our transformation to gain God's approval are considered rubbish, garbage, and altogether filthy (see Isaiah 64:6). No accomplishment in life, no sum of money, and no position can make us acceptable to God. Our "rightness" with God is found only in Christ. You don't have to change who you are. He accepts you as you are in Christ.

Read *Philippians 3:2–9.*

Why did Paul consider the accomplishments in his life as a loss? *(Because of the surpassing worth of knowing Christ.)*

What did Paul want to gain? *(Jesus Christ. Paul originally considered his good deeds as a gain, but later considered them a loss. Because Paul had no righteousness of his own, he wanted to gain Christ and be found in him.)*

We all, like Paul, have a gain and a loss column. What are you placing in either of those columns?

Prayer

Thank God that our acceptance comes from what Jesus has done for us, not what we do for him.

DAY 3

Imagine that you have been convicted of murder and find yourself standing before a judge. He is about to say that you're guilty and hand down the death penalty to you.

But just before the judge hits his gavel on the sound block, through the door storms a man. "Stop," he tells the judge. "I will gladly take the punishment that this murderer deserves."

In response to this man's offer, the judge says that you're innocent and free to go home.

This story helps illustrate one of the most important topics in the Bible: justification.

God is a holy and perfect judge. He will not overlook crimes, especially those we have committed against him. And because of our sinful condition and our wicked acts, God is right and even just to punish us. Thankfully, Jesus Christ lived, died, and rose again to take the punishment that we rightfully deserve.

Read *Romans 3:20.*

Will good works justify us before God? *(No.)*

What comes through the law? *(The knowledge of sin. We wouldn't know specifically what not to do if it weren't for the law.)*

We can only be made right before God when he declares us just. This is like a double transaction, where God takes away our sin and unrighteousness through Jesus' death in our place, and credits Jesus' righteousness in our place.

Does seeing your sin exchanged with Jesus' righteousness change the way you understand your salvation?

Prayer

Thank God that he has credited Jesus' righteousness to your life, making you right before him through Jesus' death.

DAY 4

Tom and Jerry is a classic cartoon about a cat and a mouse. These short episodes normally have Tom chasing Jerry and destroying everything in his path. But regardless of how hard he tries and how smart his tactics are, Tom never catches Jerry. In our pursuit of getting right with God, we want to make sure that we're not like Tom.

We can't make ourselves right with God. No matter how hard we try, we will never be able to win his approval. We will always fall short in our efforts.

God's acceptance of us is by grace alone, through faith alone, in Jesus Christ alone.

Our justification before God is all about Jesus. His goodness, not ours, saves us. Jesus' life, not our own, is our hope. Jesus' death, not our religious efforts was our payment. Jesus alone forgives sin, and we are to seek him and repent of our sin.

Our justification is not accomplished in any part by our own work, morality, or religious devotion. Faith in Jesus alone is what justifies us. Jesus plus anything ruins everything.

Read *Romans 5:1–3.*

Once we have been justified by faith through Jesus, what do we have with God? *(We have peace.)*

On what do we stand? *(We stand on grace, and peace with God through Jesus. This means that our position with God is securely founded upon Jesus Christ. We don't have to maintain what we haven't earned.)*

Do you think and feel that you are at peace with God through faith in Jesus? Why or why not?

Prayer

Thank God that you are at peace with him through faith in Jesus Christ. Rejoice with your family in the hope that you have in Christ.

DAY 5

The moment we are changed by the Holy Spirit to follow Christ is the moment we refer to as *regeneration*. Regeneration occurs when the Holy Spirit makes us spiritually alive so that we desire Jesus. Jesus himself called it being "born again" (John 3:1–15).

Before this occurs in our lives, we are spiritually dead. Unresponsive to God. And in our spiritual death, we have no ability to do anything in bringing us closer to God. We are like Lazarus: dead and already buried.

Yet, unlike Lazarus, who was buried in a physical tomb, we each are buried in a spiritual tomb of sin. We are dependent upon Jesus calling out our names and saying, "Come forth!" (See John 11:1–43.)

Paul described this experience in the Christian's life in Jesus as becoming a "new man," (Eph. 2:15) made "alive together with Christ," (Eph. 2:5) and "created in Christ Jesus." (Eph. 2:10) What each of these descriptions tells us about regeneration is that it is a permanent, unalterable change in us at the deepest level.

We are raised from spiritual death to life.

Read *John 3:1–18.*

What is the only way someone can see the kingdom of God? *(He or she must be born again.)*

How is someone "born again"? *(By having faith in Jesus Christ. This is not a physical rebirth, but a spiritual rebirth.)*

When you think about your life, would you say that you've been born again?

Prayer

Thank God for the work of the Holy Spirit in applying Jesus Christ's work for you and in you.

DAY 6

The writers of the New Testament were fond of comparing our old, sinful life with our Spirit-regenerated new life. They did this to clearly distinguish what our life is and is not.

Your new life in Christ is found in him alone. It can only be discovered in what he has done for you—not the messages you hear from all the competing voices in the world, at school, or even at home, but in what Christ has done to save you.

Through faith in Christ you have been crucified with him. He now lives within you and takes priority in what you do. This means that the new life you live, you live by faith in Jesus, not in what you do for Jesus (Gal. 2:20).

Read *Ephesians 4:17–24.*

How is life apart from Jesus Christ described in verses 17–19?

In what way do verses 20–24 compare our old life apart from Christ with our new life in Christ?

Prayer

Thank God that in Christ you are a new creation and that he is at work in your life.

DAY 7

Have you ever thought, *I put my faith in Jesus. Why am I not seeing more changes in my life?*

This is an understandable frustration. Many times as Christians we feel as if we're just stuck in mud and unable to make any progress. We want to keep walking forward, but our feet are stuck. The primary reason we have these experiences is that while we are made new in Christ, in this life we are not made *completely* new in Christ.

Until we meet Christ in heaven, we will live our lives with a seed of sinful rebellion from Adam in us. We will also battle against the temptations of the world and the traps of the devil. In this life we continually grow to live out of our new identity as new people in Christ through a process called *sanctification*. As we are sanctified, we learn more about Jesus and become more like him by the power of the Holy Spirit.

One day, we will die. If we die in Christ, we'll be made fully, completely, unchangingly, and eternally new. This is what theologians call *glorification*. On that day your faith will be sight, as you will be able to see the risen and reigning Jesus, face-to-face. On that day everyone in Christ will be made completely perfect, as together we rise like Jesus, to be like him together forever.

In Christ you are new. And . . . he is not done with you.

Read *Romans 8:28–30.*

What has God promised to those who love him? *(That he will work all things together for their good.)*

What is the process of our salvation in Romans 8:29–30? *(We are predestined > called > justified > glorified.)*

God isn't in the business of saving us and leaving us the same as before. From beginning to end God initiates and completes the work he starts in us (Phil 1:6). Would you say that you have entrusted your life to God from beginning to end?

Prayer

Thank God that by his grace you will persevere in your faith until the end of your life.

WEEK 12
I AM FORGIVEN

DAY 1

Imagine writing down every wrong thing you've ever done, and everything you should've done, but didn't. Add to that all the sinful thoughts, words, and motives you've ever had.

Once you were done writing down this list, you would realize that it's long. Real long.

From this list consider that every sin is a direct assault against God as the rightful Ruler and Judge of creation. God feels anger over sin, and he hates it.

Thankfully, there is good news for us because of Jesus' work on the cross. Jesus received God's wrath in our place. Through faith in Jesus the wrath of God is turned away from us, because Jesus took it for us.

In Christ you are forgiven.

Read *Hebrews 10:15–18.*

Where is God's law placed through faith in Jesus? *(On our hearts and in our minds.)*

How does God's law in our hearts and minds change the way we live our lives? *(We are compelled from the inside out to love and serve God with our lives by the power of the Holy Spirit.)*

Does God remember your sins in Christ? Is there anything you need to do if you sin to make things right with you and God? *(God will not remember our sins in Christ. Christ has fulfilled the requirements of the law for us and has taken upon himself the punishment that we deserve. This means we are forgiven in Christ for anything we do. We no do not have to offer any sacrifice or perform any particular deed to make ourselves right with God.)*

Prayer

Thank God that you are forgiven in Christ. Thank Jesus that he has fulfilled the requirements of the law for you and has taken upon himself the punishment that you deserve.

DAY 2

Rose lived in a Christian bubble. Everyone she knew identified him- or herself as a Christian. Rose's every activity revolved around her church and private Christian school.

This environment eventually led her to doubt God. She had unintentionally placed her trust in what she did, where she spent her time, and who she hung out with, instead of in Jesus. She worked hard to please God, but she was often plagued with bouts of guilt over judging others while overlooking her own sins. Since she was working to please God, she also struggled with doubts of her salvation.

Rose was humbled to see her errors and misplaced hope. Through a series of fortunate events, she repented of her religiosity and placed her trust in Jesus. Rose said of this moment, "I cannot express the overwhelming difference Jesus has made in my life." She went on to say, "I no longer have to doubt my salvation, and I have a lot more faith in Jesus and a lot less faith in myself. He sustains me now, not my unspoken list of Christians duties."

Your good works will not earn your forgiveness from God. In Christ you are forgiven. And this forgiveness is powerful.

Read Acts 7:54–60.

The apostle Paul was the ultimate legalist, bar none. He even oversaw the death of Stephen. How did Stephen respond to Paul (who was called Saul at that time) and the others who stoned him? *(He prayed that the Lord would not hold their sin against them.)*

How did God answer Stephen's prayer for Saul? *(He allowed Saul to experience the power of forgiveness. Saul became a Christian, was forgiven of all his sins—including participating in Stephen's murder—and changed his name to Paul.)*

You can illustrate this with your kids through a discussion about adoption, saying, "When a family adopts someone, that child is included in the family and given a new name. In the same way, when someone is adopted by God, he is given a new identity, and in Saul's case, a new name."

Prayer

Thank God for the power of forgiveness in your life and the lives of others.

DAY 3

Understanding the truth of God's wrath allows us to appreciate more deeply the truth of God's grace and understand the happiest words a sinner could ever hear, "God in Christ forgave you."

Are you in Christ? If so, then God has forgiven you for all of your sins—past, present, and future. Jesus Christ shouted, "It is finished," as his final words in triumphant victory from the cross. At that moment, sin was atoned for and sinners were forgiven.

Read Romans 3:21–26.

What have all people done? *(They have all sinned and fallen short of the glory of God.)*

What is God's gift to us through his grace and the redemption that is in Christ? *(We are justified. God has declared us not guilty in Christ.)*

How did God justify us through Jesus? *(He put Jesus forward as the propitiation for our sins. In Christ God's wrath has been satisfied. If we are in Christ, there is nothing we need to do to compensate for our sins.)*

If there are enough people in your family, you can act out this lesson. Let one person pretend to be a judge; another, a criminal on trial; a third act, the prosecuting attorney; and the fourth, Jesus. This can be acted out by having Jesus pay the penalty for the criminal's sin and showing that the judge, who represents God the Father, is satisfied with his payment.

Prayer

Thank Jesus that he satisfied the wrath of God on your behalf.

DAY 4

Do you like pulling weeds? If you're like most people, you probably don't. Who would? Pulling weeds is hard, backbreaking work.

What if you were asked to pull weeds and figured you would take a short-cut by using a Weed Eater instead? That way, you could do the work quicker and spend the extra time doing something fun instead.

You could do this, but there's one catch. Weeds have roots. They'll quickly grow back and even multiply.

God, through Paul, said that we only have two possible responses when it comes to those who've sinned against us: forgiveness or bitterness. And like weeds, the Bible tells us, bitterness has roots (Heb. 12:15). Consequently, when others sin against us, we can whack away at the surface—our frustrations, disappointments, anger, hurt, and sadness—or we can pull up our bitterness before it takes root. If you don't pull up the root of bitterness, it will return, deeper and taller than before, and become very difficult to pull out.

Read *Ephesians 4:32.*

How are we to act toward others? *(We are to be kind, tenderhearted, and forgiving.)*

Why are we to treat them this way? *(Because Jesus has treated us this way. He has forgiven us.)*

In dealing with the sins others have committed against us and protecting ourselves from potential bitterness, Paul encouraged us to put away lying and to instead speak the truth (Eph. 4:25). To do this we must be honest about some of our most painful memories. We must ask soul-searching questions and get beyond simply saying we're fine. Is there anyone who has sinned against you that you need to lovingly and truthfully approach?

Prayer

Ask God for the grace and power of the Holy Spirit to help you and your family to forgive, since Jesus has forgiven us.

DAY 5

Do you harbor bitterness in your heart when things don't work out as expected or someone mistreats you? If so, you may be in danger.

Paul was clear in Ephesians 4:31–32 that if bitterness isn't exchanged for forgiveness, it escalates and becomes increasingly devastating to both you and others. He listed the steps that proceed from bitterness: wrath, anger, clamor, slander, and malice (ESV).

When we're *bitter*, we refuse to forgive.

Next *wrath* develops; we become irritated, agitated, and we can feel our blood pressure rising.

Unrighteous *anger* proceeds not from injustice, but rather, from our continued bitterness. This causes us to be furious with our offenders and motivated to harm them in some way.

Clamor can be heard when our anger is no longer contained and we begin to engage in a noisy conflict with others.

Slander occurs when, in an effort to vindicate ourselves and vilify others, we gossip about them and seek to ruin their reputations.

Malice is evident when we begin to invent ways of doing evil to punish those against whom we're bitter, regardless of personal cost. The entire goal is to make our offenders lose, even if that should mean we lose as well. At the point of malice, people are capable of horrific evil and out-of-character conduct that is oftentimes hard to even imagine.

In Christ you are forgiven, so in him, exchange the bitterness you feel with his peace. This is the only way to ultimately break the cycle of bitterness.

Read *Ephesians 4:31.*

What are we to do with all bitterness, wrath, anger, clamor, slander, and malice? *(Put them away from us.)*

Why would God ask us to "put away" these characteristics?

How do we "put away" these things?

Prayer

Ask God to make you and your family aware of any cycle of bitterness. Thank him that in Christ you are forgiven and that you can forgive and break the cycle of bitterness in your own life and your family's lives.

DAY 6

As Jesus entered the Jewish temple prior to his crucifixion, he observed something terrible happening. The Temple had been turned into a mall. Local merchants had set up their businesses and were making a profit on Temple property. This made Jesus furious. In response, he flipped over their tables and drove them out of the temple. Yet, even in his anger, Jesus did not sin.

It's not always a sin to be angry. There are appropriate times to feel and express anger. Yet, many times people tell us that we shouldn't feel that way about the wrongs we've suffered. This type of counsel is both unbiblical and unhelpful.

God has a long wick and is slow to anger. But we are told throughout the Bible that God does get angry in response to sin.

Righteous anger is the right response to sin. This is a far more consistent response with the character of God than faking happiness, approval, or acceptance. The Bible, on many occasions, gives us examples of human anger that is justified. This is why Paul *didn't* say, "Don't be angry," but rather, said, "Be angry, and do not sin."

Paul accepted anger as a legitimate emotional response to sin. But he also warned us to be careful not to accept or empower anger that comes from our own sin. Instead, he said, we should harness the energy of our anger toward righteousness rather than letting it fuel our descent into clamor, slander, and malice.

Read Ephesians 4:26–27.

How quickly are we to deal with anger in our lives? *(As soon as possible. God, through Paul, said to not "let the sun go down on your anger"* [ESV].*)*

Why do you think God wants us to deal with anger so promptly? *(The devil is capable of leveraging anger in our lives and using it for his purposes. This is why Paul warned us to "give no opportunity to the devil"* [esv].*)*

What has your response been to anger in your life?

Prayer

Thank God that Jesus died for the anger in your life and that Jesus, not your anger, identifies you. Ask for his help in dealing with any anger as soon as possible.

DAY 7

Trash-talking. Name-calling. Bad-mouthing. Each of these is a way to insult others. And if we're honest, we've all been guilty of insulting someone else at some point in time.

The words that come out of our mouths serve as a way of testing our hearts to see what is in them. You can quickly tell what someone is feeling by just listening to what comes out of his or her mouth. If someone is bitter, he'll most likely insult others. If he feels forgiven, he'll probably forgive others.

By God's grace give your bitterness to Jesus in exchange for his forgiveness. When you receive his forgiveness, be quick to extend it to others.

Read *Proverbs 18:21 (esv); James 3:1–5.*

To what is the tongue compared in James 3? *(Horses' bits and ships' rudders.)*

Why did James compare the tongue to these small objects? *(The tongue is also small, and yet, like these small things, it is powerful in what it can do for good or bad.)*

How do you use your tongue? For good, or evil?

Prayer

Ask God to empower you to use your tongue for good and for praising him. If you have used your tongue in a way that is displeasing to God, repent of those sins.

WEEK 13
I AM ADOPTED

DAY 1

The young boy Benjamin was packed into a small orphanage room filled with cribs and fatherless children. He rarely got to go outside and play, and called the only man working at the orphanage—a security guard—Father.

Benjamin is one of six million orphans in his nation. His story is tragically common in a country ravaged by famine and poverty. His mother, a poor peasant, gave birth to Benjamin in a culture that views him as worthless because he has no father and will not inherit land.

That Benjamin even ended up in an orphanage is an act of God's grace. His mother, faced with pressure from the family and no way to provide for the boy, wished to take Benjamin to the forest, lay him down, and simply leave him there to die. By God's grace, the tribal elders of her village prevented her actions for fear that the government would find out and they would get in trouble. And by God's grace a family adopted Benjamin.

Commenting on this process, the adoptive father said, "Benjamin was doomed, and nothing of his own doing. And he could not save himself. Someone needed to save him."

Just as Benjamin was adopted by his new earthly father, we have been adopted by our spiritual Father in Christ.

Read *Ephesians 5:1–2.*

What are we to be? *(Imitators of God.)*

Why are we capable of being imitators of God? *(Because he is our father and we are his children. Just as children, even adopted ones, can imitate their earthly parents, so can we imitate God.)*

Prayer

Thank God that he is your Father and that you are his child in Christ.

DAY 2

Adoption is not a recent practice in history. Christians have adopted children since the time of Christ.

During the time in which Jesus lived, children in the Roman Empire were often severely beaten and even tossed out into the garbage or on a dung heap to either die or be taken by someone and used as slaves, prostitutes, gladiators, or worse. Living in this culture of abandonment, Christians, many of them poor, started doing something countercultural: they began adopting "throw-away" children as family, loving them, and nurturing them.

Why would Christians do this? The answer to this question is seen in Paul's comparison of the gospel to adoption. We were once "sons of disobedience," but now we're "heirs with Christ." Adoptive parents in Jesus' time wanted *heirs*.

So does God.

Read *Romans 8:12–17.*

Who are considered the sons and daughters of God? *(Those who are led by the Spirit of God.)*

Why are those who are led by God's Spirit considered part of his family? *(They have received the Spirit of adoption, and now they call him Father.)*

What do you inherit as a child of God? *(His promises.)*

Do you sense that you are a son or daughter of God? Do you have a desire to call him Father?

Prayer

Thank God that he has adopted you into his family and has given you an inheritance.

DAY 3

A father is one of the most significant influences in a person's life. So much in life is determined by who one's father is, how he behaves, and how present he is or isn't.

Thankfully, regardless of how amazing or absent our fathers are, in Christ we have a new and perfect Father in heaven who has adopted us into his family. We have inherited his resources, and he has transformed our entire life and destiny. Since we are now part of his family, our lives will be vastly different than they would have been apart from him.

Adoption is a legal matter. Children cannot declare themselves part of any family. The family has to decide to legally adopt children. Many families gladly and lovingly do.

The point is, just as an orphan can't force his way into an earthly family, neither can we force our way into God's family. Rather, God the Father lovingly adopts us as his sons and daughters through the work of our big brother Jesus.

Now that you're a Christian, God the Father has freely chosen to spiritually adopt, love, and bless you. If you didn't have a good earthly father, you now have a perfect heavenly Father. And if you did have a good earthly father, you now have the additional blessing of your perfect heavenly father.

Read *Ephesians 1:2–3, 17; 2:18; 3:14; 4:6; 5:20; 6:23.*

Read through these passages together. Discuss what they have to say about God the Father.

Prayer

Thank God the Father for gladly, willingly, and lovingly adopting you into his family through Christ.

DAY 4

Ephesians 1:5 says that we have been "adopt[ed] as sons by Jesus Christ." In an age when some wonder if there are other saviors and paths to salvation, we must never forget that our spiritual adoption is solely "by Jesus Christ." There is no other path or savior by which we can be saved. God the Father has chosen to only adopt and save those who are in Christ.

Someone once said, "The God of the Bible has no 'natural' or 'begotten' children apart from Jesus the Son; all the rest of us need to be adopted."[2] Jesus knew this, and he promised that he would accomplish our adoption. In Christ alone we're adopted and receive all the benefits and blessings that are his because he has graciously chosen to share them with us.

This is why Jesus is both the Son of God and our big brother.

Read *John 20:16–17.*

To whom did Jesus tell Mary to go? *(To his brothers.)*

To whom was Jesus ascending? *(His Father and your Father.)*

What do the answers to these questions say about Jesus' relationship with us?

Prayer

Thank Jesus that he is both the Son of God and your brother.

DAY 5

When a child is adopted by a family, many times he or she is becomes part of a family with brothers and sisters. In the same way, when God the Father adopts us spiritually, we're adopted into a family with other brothers and sisters. As Christians, we are part of an extended family.

This may not seem like a big deal, but when you consider the biblical language of family used in the New Testament, it takes on a whole new meaning. During the time when Paul wrote Ephesians, it may have been illegal to call someone a close relative, such as brother or sister, if that individual was not legally related to you. To simply call someone your brother or sister would run the risk of confusing the inheritance rights that were only to be distributed to close family members upon someone's death.

For the Christian; however, sometimes our relationships in the family of God are even closer than those of blood relatives. Many early Christians saw their brothers and sisters in Christ as the primary designation for their identity and risked losing the inheritance from their biological families.

This goes to show that our "family in Christ" is not just a feel-good label we use, or something we take for granted. In a very real and tangible way, in Christ we are adopted into the family of God and have new brothers and sisters.

Read 1 John 3:1–3.

What has God called you, and what are you right now in Christ? *(According to 1 John 3:1–2 you are called and considered a child of God.)*

Right now, in Christ, you are a child of God. This means that anyone else who is in Christ is also God's child and is considered your brother or sister. Does this change the way you relate with others in Christ? Why or why not?

Prayer

Thank God for adopting you into his family and giving you new brothers and sisters in Christ. Ask for his help in being the brother or sister in Christ that he has called you to be.

DAY 6

Adopted children share in the joys and blessings of being a part of their new families. One of the many benefits they receive is the right to an eventual inheritance. This is also true for those who are adopted by God the Father in Christ.

Unlike earthly inheritances that may not exist or may be reduced by the loss of money or possessions, our inheritance promised by God is guaranteed.

In Christ, God the Father has adopted you, and you have obtained an inheritance (Eph. 1:11). This is no ordinary inheritance. It isn't passed down from family to family. It isn't based on our employment or investments. The inheritance promised to us is the hope of the life to come (Eph. 1:18).

Even though the many promises we have made and the promises made by others have not been kept, God always keeps his promises. As Ephesians 1:13–14 says, we are "sealed with the Holy Spirit of promise, who is the guarantee of our inheritance until the redemption of the purchased possession, to the praise of His glory."

In Christ you have a new inheritance: the hope of the life to come in heaven.

Read *Ephesians 1:11, 13–14, 18; 3:6; 5:5.*

What do these passages say about your inheritance as an adopted child of God?

Whoever is leading the devotion, pray Ephesians 1:18, "having the eyes of your hearts enlightened, that you may know what is the hope to which he has called you, what are the riches of his glorious inheritance in the saints" (ESV).

DAY 7

The color of your skin, eyes, and hair, and even your height are determined by who your parents are. Your family also plays an important role in who you are as a person. They even influence your outlook on life and the way you behave. Even so, your parents and family are not where you ultimately find your identity.

God has created you in his image, and in Christ you are adopted into the family of God. Your adoption in Christ transforms everything about who you are and what you do.

In Christ you enter into an intimate relationship with God the Father, a relationship so close and personal that it's similar to the relationship Jesus shares with him. As a child of your Father, you can approach him for anything and everything.

Because you are adopted into God's family, your life is transformed. You are a new creation in Christ (2 Cor. 5:17). As such, you are called to live a life that imitates God the Father, represents the family name, and reflects Jesus.

Thankfully, God doesn't leave us alone in this pursuit. We are empowered by the Holy Spirit to live out our new identity in Christ.

Read *Ephesians 5:1–21.*

As children of God, we imitate God. These verses are best understood as describing our new identity in Christ. What is described here characterizes how we are to live as children of God. Have everyone go through these verses* and do two things:

First, have them identify the good things we should do. *(Imitate God [v. 1]; walk in love [v. 2]; walk as children of light [v. 8]; discern what pleases God [v. 10]; walk wisely [5:15]; make the best use of our time [v. 16]; be filled with the Spirit [v. 18]; sing to one another and to the Lord [v. 19]; give thanks [vv. 4, 20].)*

Second, have them identify the evil things we should avoid. *(Sexual immorality, impurity, and covetousness [v. 3]; filthiness, foolish talk, and crude humor [v. 4]; association with those who are sexually immoral or covetous [v. 7]; works of darkness [v. 11]; drunkenness [v. 18].)*

*From the ESV's rendering.

As you look through what we should embrace and avoid, how do your actions compare?

Prayer

Thank God for giving you a new identity as a member of his family. Ask to be filled with the Holy Spirit so you will be empowered to live your new life in Christ.

WEEK 14
I AM LOVED

DAY 1

Kimberly was born into a family where her mom and dad abused alcohol and each other. They constantly yelled at and physically hurt one another. "I thought 'love' was when you beat on each other and yelled all the time," says Kimberly.

Eventually her parents both had affairs and divorced, leaving Kimberly's mother to raise her and her four younger siblings alone.

After the divorce Kimberly's mother went through eight more marriages and eventually kicked Kimberly out of the house when she turned fifteen. Shy, scared, and alone, Kimberly fell in love with the first boy who paid attention to her. When she turned sixteen, she found herself homeless, pregnant, and feeling worthless and unloved.

Kimberly's life was radically changed when a friend from her past invited her to spend the night. That evening her friend told her about Christ's love for her.

Over the years Kimberly grew in the grace and knowledge of Jesus Christ. Her life has undergone a miraculous transformation. Kimberly's old friends wouldn't even recognize the woman she is today. She is happily married, with six kids, and most important, Kimberly is loved by Jesus.

Jesus loves you too.

Read *1 John 4:15–17.*

What did John come to "know and believe"? *(The love that God has for him. John was assured that God loved him and that Jesus had died for him.)*

How is love perfected? *(Love is perfected by our abiding, our continuing, in the love of God. Our love for God and others is an expression of God's love for us.)*

Are you assured of God's love for you? Why or why not?

Thank God for his love for you and your family.

DAY 2

Today, love is celebrated as a god. Nearly every movie, book, and television show has a love story. These plots aren't complicated. Typically, those in love are faced with some relational difficulty, which is ultimately resolved in a happy ending.

These stories pick up on something about how we're wired as human beings. We're wired to avoid tension and to long for peace. But you probably already know that life isn't like the stories we read and watch.

Most of us are loved by a handful of people. Many others go through life loved by no one at all. Regardless of who does and does not love us, we all long to be loved.

To satisfy this longing, people look for love from others. What we soon discover is that we will never find complete satisfaction in the love others provide. There will always exist a deeper longing. Thankfully, there is one person who can satisfy our deepest longings for love perfectly, completely, and forever.

In Christ you are perfectly loved. In him your longing for loved is satisfied.

Read *Ephesians 5:25–33.*

Find every reference to *love* in these verses. *(There are six: two in verse 25, three in verse 28, and one in verse 33.)*

What do these references tell you about love? How does this compare to the portrayal of love today? *(The love mentioned here is unconditional and irrevocable. It involves more than just feelings. It is displayed perfectly in action—sometimes despite our feelings. Today's "love" is overwhelmingly based on feelings and is rarely considered unconditional and irrevocable.)*

Do you believe Jesus loves you unconditionally?

How can you best portray this type of love to others?

Thank Jesus for his perfect love for you. Pray that you and your family can comprehend the breadth, length, height, and depth of Jesus' love for you that surpasses all understanding (Eph. 3:18–19 ESV).

DAY 3

Karl Barth was a Bible teacher known to have stood up to Adolf Hitler in Germany during the height of World War II.

During the 1960s, Dr. Barth visited the United States to lecture at Yale, Princeton, and the University of Chicago. Large crowds came out to hear him speak.

During this speaking tour, a reporter asked Dr. Barth what was the single most important theological discovery he'd made. After stopping to consider his answer carefully, Barth said, "Jesus loves me. This I know, for the Bible tells me so."

Jesus' love for us is much more than a cliché or a bumper sticker slogan. Jesus' love for you and the church is the foundation of the Christian faith.

Read *1 John 4:9–10.*

How was God's love for us manifested? In other words, how did he show how much he loves you and me? *(God sent his only Son into the world to die on our behalf.)*

Do these verses say that we were seeking God's love? *(No. They say that we have not loved God, but in spite of our lack of affection, God loved us anyway.)*

How important is Jesus' love for you? Do you take his love for granted? Or is his love for you the foundation of your faith?

Prayer

Thank God for loving and seeking you in spite of your lack of love for him.

DAY 4

A bride and groom is an amazing picture of love. In the Bible, Jesus' love for the church, which includes everyone in Christ, is described as a groom's love for his bride. Next time you're at a wedding, pass a bridal magazine, or see a couple in love, take it as an opportunity to remember that Christ loves you as a groom loves his bride.

Jesus is the only one who can provide the perfect love you need. Only he can meet your deep longing for love. Once you know the love of Jesus, you can stop using people for their love and start loving them in return.

Read Ephesians 5:22–33.

How are husbands to love their wives? *(They are to love their wives as Christ loved the church by giving himself up sacrificially for her.)*

How are wives to love their husbands? *(Wives are to love their husbands by submitting to them, for the husband is the head of the wife as Christ is head of the church.)*

Marriage between one man and one woman is a picture of Jesus' love for the church. In other words, marriage is analogous to the gospel. How does this influence the way you think marriage between one man and one woman should look?

Prayer

Thank Jesus for giving himself up for the church. Ask for God's grace in helping you see marriage as a picture of the gospel.

DAY 5

It's the middle of the afternoon, and you're hungry. Feeling these hunger pangs causes you to think back on your rushed morning.

You hit the snooze button on your alarm and slept in. You left yourself with just enough time to take a quick shower, get your clothes on, and brush your teeth. You didn't have enough time to eat breakfast, let alone pack your lunch, and by noon, you're famished.

Every one of us is familiar with hunger pangs, but have you ever thought about how we can also experience love hunger?

When you believe you're unloved, you may become so desperate, hungry, and needy for love that you will use people to meet your longing, much as you consume food to satisfy your hunger. If you're like this, then you may even put up with those who abuse you. You're constantly in a romantic relationship or have a best friendship to avoid the risk of becoming emotionally undone.

The Bible calls this idolatry. This is turning a good thing into a god thing. Rather than letting Jesus be your all, you become so addicted to relationships that you make an idol out of someone else's love. The problem with idols is that they always fail us.

But Jesus never fails. He showers us with perfect love, and just being with him brings joy and pleasure.

Read *Psalm 16:11.*

What does God make known to us? *(The path of life.)*

What do we experience in God's presence, and what is at his right hand? *(In his presence we experience fullness of joy, and at his right hand are pleasures forevermore.)*

The path God reveals to us leads us to his presence through Christ. In Christ you can seek and experience the fullness of joy and the pleasures spoken of here. Do you seek joy and pleasure in Christ?

Is there anything that distracts you from pursuing joy and pleasure in Christ?

Prayer

Thank God for revealing to you his path of life through Christ. Ask for his grace in pursuing him and in experiencing the joy and pleasure that only he can provide.

DAY 6

In 1964, the Righteous Brothers belted out their now-famous line, "You've lost that lovin' feelin'." Although the song was a smash hit nearly fifty years ago, it still captures the heart of people's thoughts on love today.

When it comes to love, many of us are ruled by our feelings. You'll see and hear of people falling out of love or losing that loving feeling. This leads to leaving your boyfriend or girlfriend, or even your spouse, in search for that next high of feeling "in love."

In the end, a person ruled by emotions becomes a type of love junkie who has become more and more tolerant of that addictive feeling and will constantly be in and out of relationships. Unfortunately, many of us take this idea of love and apply it to God, assuming that he can quickly stop loving us depending on how we act toward him.

Thankfully, God's love for us is not based on a "lovin' feelin.'" His love for the church is expressed as unconditional and irrevocable, the type of love that should exist between a groom and his bride. It is displayed perfectly in action, not feeling, and sometimes even *despite* feeling.

In Christ you are unconditionally loved.

Read 1 John 4:7–12.

What is God, according to verse 8? *(God is love.)*

How does God show us he loves us? *(God sent his only Son into the world so that we could live.)*

How are we to respond to God's sacrificial love? *(We are to love one another as God loves us. That means that our love must be more than just a feeling. Our love, like God's, must be rooted in sacrificial service.)*

How have you responded to God's love?

Does seeing God's love as constant and unchanging give you security in your relationship with him through Christ?

Prayer

Thank God that his love is constant, unchanging, and unconditional. Ask for his help in moving you to love others as Jesus has loved you.

DAY 7

Do you struggle accepting God's love for you? If so, don't feel alone. Many do.

Sometimes the weight and burden of our sins causes us to lose sight of our identity in Christ and the fact that God actually and personally loves us. We may believe that God loves the world, or individual people in it, but we're less likely to believe that God loves *us*. This is because we struggle to accept that God's love is pure, unmerited, and free grace.

Today, understand that Jesus loves you. He cannot love you any more than he already does. He will not love you any less. Jesus has laid down his life for you.

Read *1 John 4:18–21.*

Why do we often fear? *(We think we will be punished.)*

Is there any fear in love? *(No.)*

Why is there no fear in love? *(Perfect love casts out fear, and we know that God's love for us is perfect because he sent Jesus Christ to die for us.)*

In Christ God loves you. There is no need to fear any punishment. In Christ the punishment you deserve has been paid for, yesterday, today, and tomorrow. Do you live your life in Christ as if he has paid the penalty for every sin you will ever commit?

Prayer

Thank Jesus for taking the punishment you deserve for your sins. Ask for God's help in accepting his sacrifice for you so that you may experience his love more fully.

WEEK 15
I AM REWARDED

DAY 1

In his book *The 360° Leader*, John Maxwell shares the story of General George Marshall, who was an important leader in World War II. Marshall worked tirelessly behind the scenes under President Roosevelt in arranging many of the strategies for victory.

As a member of the military, Marshall had a deep understanding of authority and submission to it. He also understood that he was serving a greater cause than himself. Those in authority rewarded his faithful service time and time again with promotions and praise.

Likewise, Paul promises us that as we labor under authority, both in this world and for God, we will receive just rewards for our faithfulness and effort. In Christ we are rewarded.

Read Matthew 25:14–30.

What did the man in the parable give his three servants? *(He gave them talents—or money—to invest for him.)*

What did the servants do with their talents? *(The first two servants doubled their talents. The last servant hid his.)*

What did the man do with the servants when he returned? *(He rewarded those who doubled their talents and punished the one who didn't.)*

Prayer

Thank God that you have been entrusted with talents—in terms of both money and gifting—to be used under his supervision. Ask for his guidance in how you can best serve him.

DAY 2

Through Paul, God encourages those in and under authority to live in such a way that he can reward them both in this life and the life to come. This is precisely what is meant by Ephesians 6:8, which says, "Whatever good anyone does, he will receive the same from the Lord."

Many Christian leaders and teachers often neglect to speak much about God rewarding faithfulness because they fear that people will become self-righteous, proud, and religiously competitive, trying to outperform one another. While this is a legitimate concern, the Bible teaches repeatedly that God does in fact reward the works of faithful believers as a way of encouraging them to persevere in holiness and faithfulness, knowing that the God who loves them sees and knows all and will reward every act of obedience.

Read Matthew 5:11–12; 6:19–21; Luke 6:35; 1 Corinthians 3:13–14.

Discuss what today's Bible passages say about God's rewards.

How do these promises encourage you to live for Jesus today?

Prayer

Thank God that he is a God who rewards. Ask for his help in living more for his eternal rewards than for temporary gain.

DAY 3

When we discuss the rewards God provides, it's easy to think he "rewards" us with salvation according to our good deeds. This thought can't be farther from the truth. The Bible is very clear that we do not earn salvation as a reward for our efforts or good works. We are saved by grace through faith in Jesus Christ. Salvation is about what he has done, not about what we do.

Even though your good works do not save you, you are *still to do them.* That is what you were created for (Eph. 2:10). And as you do good works in response to what Jesus has done for you, God sees them and will reward you for them.

Read *2 Corinthians 5:9–10.*

What was Paul's aim in life? *(To please Jesus Christ.)*

Why did Paul make it his aim to please Jesus? *(He knew that he would one day appear before him and that he would receive from Jesus what was due to him, whether it was good or evil.)*

You could illustrate this by using a target. Our aim is to hit the target, especially the bull's-eye. In the same way our aim in life, the "bulls-eye" we are shooting for, should be to please Jesus Christ.

Prayer

Thank God that you have passed from death to life and will not undergo a final judgment. Ask for his help in living for his eternal rewards.

DAY 4

Why do you value the gospel? Do you value it because it meets your desire for forgiveness, health, peace, or eternal life? Although these are benefits provided through the gospel in varying degrees now and totally in heaven, they are actually not reasons why we should value and believe the gospel.

You may be thinking, *How could you say such a thing? How can eternal life not be a motive for placing my faith in Christ?*

Simple. Eternal life is not the *real* reward. So what *is* the reward? What's missing from the benefits listed above?

God himself.

The apostle John wrote: "This is eternal life, that they know you the only true God, and Jesus Christ whom you have sent" (John 17:3 ESV). Eternal life, then, is knowing, enjoying, and experiencing a relationship with God through Jesus Christ in the power of the Holy Spirit. In the words of John Piper, "God is the Gospel."[3]

The greatest reward given to us by God is the gift of himself. If you are in Christ, then you are allowed to experience a taste of eternal life now by knowing the only true God, and Jesus Christ, whom he sent. In Christ you are given the gift of God himself.

DAILY DEVOTIONS

Read Matthew 5:11–12; 6:19–21; Luke 6:35;
1 Corinthians 3:13–14.

As you read through the different rewards in these passages, what do you think about them? How do they make you feel?

Are you excited about having the reward of knowing God himself? Why or why not?

Prayer

Thank God that eternal life is knowing the one true and living God and Jesus Christ, whom he sent. Ask to come into a greater knowing of who he is.

DAY 5

Curiously, when speaking of God's rewards, Paul was writing to those who were under authority—in particular, children.

In Ephesians 6:1–2, children are commanded to "obey" and "honor" their parents. This directive was originally given in the Ten Commandments in Exodus 20 and is the first and only commandment that comes with a promise.

Children who keep this command are not given just any ordinary promise. Ephesians 6:2–3 says, "Honor your father and mother . . . that it may be well with you and you may live long on the earth." The two rewards mentioned here are remarkable and highly motivating. Put simply, God promises every believing child that obeying his or her parents, or even guardians, will lead to well-being and long life.

A child's obedience to his parents does not earn his salvation. But his obedience, or lack of it, is *revealing* of his salvation. In other words, a child's obedience to Mom and Dad reveals the genuineness and depth of his or her relationship with God. This is also true of everyone who is under the authority of others.

Whether we are children, students, employees, or athletes, we are under someone's authority. In our submission to God's authority in our lives, we are to be submissive to other authorities in our lives. This doesn't mean that we are passive or even pushovers. What it means is that we glorify God in our obedience to and honor of those in authority over us.

Read *Ephesians 6:1–9.*

Why do you think our submission to authority is important? *(It is revealing of our submission to God's authority in our lives. If we are not submissive to the earthly authorities in our lives, then we are more than likely not submitted to God's authority either.)*

Who is in authority over you, and how are you responding?

Do you sense any conviction of sin in light of what Paul wrote and to whom he wrote it?

Prayer

Thank God for the authority figures in your life. Ask him to reveal any sin in your life with regard to how you submit to authority.

DAY 6

Have you ever served in a position of leadership in school, sports, or even extracurricular activities? If so, then God has entrusted you with authority over others.

Authority is a precious honor that must be stewarded well. It's not something we take advantage of. Thankfully, God provides us with commands to guide us in the way we lead people, and he will even reward us in our role. In Ephesians 6:1–4 Paul used parents, especially fathers, as an example of how God does this.

Fathers are told, "Do not provoke your children to wrath, but bring them up in the training and admonition of the Lord" (v. 4). What we see is that fathers are not supposed to act harshly toward their children, demean them, neglect them, or harm them in any way. Fathers are meant to be a blessing from the Lord to their children by taking responsibility to raise them. Every father is called to be a blessing to his children as Pastor Dad, actively involved in the development of each child's growth, with love, humility, and wisdom.

The Bible serves as our road map for life. Within its pages God has revealed his will for us in our pursuit of glorifying and enjoying him forever.

In your desire to steward your authority over others well, read, study, and memorize the Bible. When your mind is transformed by God's Word, then you will be able to know "the will of God, what is good and acceptable and perfect" (Rom. 12:2 ESV).

Read *Ephesians 6:1–9.*

How are fathers to treat those under their authority?

Over whom do you have authority at work, home, church, or any other place?

How would those under your authority say you treat them?

Prayer

Thank Jesus that he has served you by dying for your sins. Ask for his help to serve those under your authority in a way that he has served you.

DAY 7

Has there ever been a time when you feared someone else's opinion? If you're not sure, think about this: Were you ever embarrassed or made to feel terrible by someone's opinion? Were you crushed when you found out somebody didn't accept your friend request on Facebook? These are just a couple of examples that reveal whether or not we fear the opinions of others. Fearing others can be devastating in our efforts to live for Jesus.

We live with either the fear of God or the fear of man. It's impossible to live fearing both God and someone else at the same time. Whom we fear determines what we do and how we live.

The fear of man is vision without hope, and it turns us into false prophets seeing only a bleak and dreaded future. This type of fear is about not getting what we want, getting what we do want but losing it, or getting what we don't want.

The answer to the fear, or *dread*, of man is the fear, or *respect*, of God. In fact . . . 150 times. That means that we are not to live our lives afraid of what others may think of us or do to us. Instead, we are to live in awe and reverence of God alone.

In other words, rather than fearing man, the Bible commands us to have a healthy fear of God. This means we care more about what he says than what others say, and we serve him tirelessly, knowing that he will reward us for being faithful. Paul affirmed this, commanding us to work "not with eye service, as men-pleasers, but as bondservants of Christ, doing the will of God from the heart, with goodwill doing service, as to the Lord, and not to men, knowing that whatever good anyone does, he will receive the same from the Lord" (Eph. 6:6–8).

Read *Proverbs 29:25.*

What does having the fear of man do in our lives? *(It lays a snare, or trap, in our lives.)*

What are we promised if we trust in the Lord? *(We are promised safety.)*

Whom, or what, do you fear?

Prayer

If anyone in your family has expressed fear in his or her life, pray that God will deliver your loved one from that fear. Thank him that we our safe in Christ.

WEEK 16
I AM VICTORIOUS

DAY 1

Imagine how terrifying being kidnapped would be. You're tied up and unable to flee your captor's grasp. Your only hope of escape is if your family and friends pay the ransom demanded for your life.

Each and every one of us has been abducted—only, we have been abducted by something much more sinister than a man. We are born with a sinful nature that has taken us captive. And worse, as sin's hostages, we have committed various sinful acts that deserve the just punishment of God.

Thankfully, we have a hero who has come to redeem us.

To be redeemed is to be released by someone upon receiving a payment. This act of redemption is just like the illustration above. We are in need of someone to pay our ransom. Jesus himself paid our ransom and delivered us from sin's grasp.

Unfortunately many of us live our lives as if Christ paid the ransom but then left us with our abductor, still in captivity and held against our wills. Jesus not only paid the ransom for sin; he redeemed us from its grasp. In Christ you have been redeemed from the power of sin.

We are enslaved to sin. Our very nature shackles us to its passions and desires. We are under its power and influence.

Jesus has redeemed you from the power of sin. Sin no longer serves as your master, and you are no longer its slave.

In Christ you are victorious. You have been emancipated from the penalty and power of sin in your life.

Read *Colossians 2:13–15.*

Apart from Christ you are considered spiritually dead. According to verse 15, what has God done to address this? *(God has made you alive with him by forgiving you of every single one of your sins. This means that spiritually you are no longer dead in your sin but have been given new desires to seek God,)*

How did God do this for you? *(Jesus canceled the record of our debt by nailing it to the cross.)*

What did Jesus do to the spiritual rulers and authorities who are against us? *(He disarmed them and put them to open and public shame by triumphing over them at the cross.)*

Prayer

Thank Jesus for his victory over Satan and sin. Since he has defeated them both, you now enjoy victory and will experience a complete victory over Satan and sin in heaven. Make sure to thank him for that too!

DAY 2

Have you ever had one of those days when everything went wrong? From things breaking, to your tripping over something, shutting your finger in a door, getting a bad grade on a test, or making a mistake during a game, nothing goes right and everything goes wrong? We all have. What's more, some of us have been really sick or lost a loved one. These times cause us to pause and think, *Why does life have to be so hard?*

The answer to this question is that there's an enemy who hates God, hates you, and has set his army against you because you're in Christ.

God loves you, but Satan hates you. God plans good for you, but Satan plots to destroy you. As a Christian you are a soldier in a war.

When we don't know or we forget that life is a war and Satan is our enemy, we can't make sense of the struggles we face. When troubles come, we are tempted to blame them on God's judgment. In reality the bad things in our lives are often an attack from our enemy—or the results of our following him through sin or our own bad choices.

The good news is that rather than God judging us, he poured out his wrath on Jesus, who secured a victory over Satan, sin, and death for us on the cross. The next time you find that things aren't going well at all, take your eyes off of what's going on and place them on Jesus.

Read *1 Peter 1:3–9.*

According to Peter, why are we to rejoice? *(Even though we have trials from time to time, we rejoice because we have been born again to a living hope and given an imperishable inheritance in heaven.)*

Why does God permit trials in his children's lives? *(Trials test the genuineness of our faith and refine us, resulting in praise to Jesus.)*

To avoid or ignore suffering in our life is to miss out on one of the reasons God allows us to experience it. Our faith is tested. By enduring our trials through God's grace, we are found to be genuine in our belief of Jesus. How have you responded to suffering in your life?

Prayer

Thank Jesus that he suffered on your behalf and that by his grace you, too, can endure suffering and trials.

DAY 3

In 1940, the Nazi regime commissioned the famed *Bismarck*, the largest battleship in the world. It had eight guns that held shells fifteen inches across, as well as some five dozen other weapons. Its targeting system was so accurate that it destroyed the Royal Navy's most prized ship with a single shot. As amazing as the *Bismarck* was, however, it had one small, but fatal, weakness.

The *Bismarck* had a vulnerable rudder. In the darkness of night the Royal Navy attacked the ship with little success—until one torpedo hit this rudder. The boat was left dead in the water, attacked fiercely, and eventually defeated.

The key to victory in war is knowing your enemy. If you don't know your enemy, you can't know how to attack them or defend yourself. The Royal Navy found the *Bismarck*'s weakness, but it took many battles and heavy losses. Imagine how many lives and ships would've been saved had they known the *Bismarck*'s weakness before it was even launched.

In this life, we have to know our enemy's weakness so we can both defend ourselves and confront our enemy to be victorious.

Read *Ephesians 6:10–12.*

Why are we to put on the whole armor of God? *(So we can defend ourselves against the schemes, or plans. of the devil.)*

What exactly are we battling when we engage in warfare with the devil? *(Our struggles are not with flesh and blood, but against the rulers, authorities, cosmic powers, and the spiritual forces of evil in the heavenly places* [ESV]*)*

Do you make a lot or little of the devil in your life? That is, do you blame everything on him, or give him no credit at all? Where are you imbalanced in your view of spiritual warfare, and why?

Prayer

Thank God for revealing your true enemy to you. Praise God that he equips you to defend yourself against his schemes.

DAY 4

It's difficult to defend yourself when you don't know who your attacker is and how he plans on attacking you. If you didn't know any better, you could end up defending yourself with a knife at a gunfight.

The Bible speaks of Satan's attacks as what can commonly be understood as *ordinary* work and *extraordinary* work. Ordinary demonic work entices us to embrace sexual sin, false religion with false teaching about a false Jesus, drunkenness, idle gossiping, lying, and idolatry. Extraordinary demonic work against us includes torment, physical injury, counterfeit miracles, accusation, death, and interaction with demons.

Christians may be deceived, accused, or tempted by Satan, and may yield to those attacks. If we wrongly respond to such attacks, we may give demons influence in our life.

As children of God, regenerated and indwelt by the Holy Spirit, we're empowered and commanded by God to resist Satan. If we do, we need not suffer from our enemy's influence. As a child of God you are never under the ruling authority of darkness, because of Jesus' victory secured for us on the cross. In Christ, we have the ability to resist our enemy, and when we do, he must flee.

Knowing how Satan fights against you will best prepare you to face whatever he throws your way.

Read *1 Peter 5:8–9.*

How did Peter want us to act? *(He wanted us to be sober-minded and watchful* [ESV]*.)*

How is the devil described? *(As a roaring lion, who prowls around, looking for someone to devour.)*

What do we learn from Peter about how the devil fights us? *(That he works through the suffering in our lives to tempt us to succumb to his ways.)*

Prayer

Thank God that according to 1 Peter 1:5 you are guarded by his power against the devil.

DAY 5

You will get tired when competing in a game. When a competition starts, you will be full of energy and excitement. But as time goes on, you'll begin to lose your strength and speed because you've been battling with your opponent. Often, most games are won in the last few minutes. The team that is able to fight with all their strength and might until the end of the game will likely win.

In your fight with your enemy Satan, you will grow weary. Thankfully, in this battle we don't go about it in our own strength. God is at work in and for us.

As a Christian soldier at war with Satan, you need learn how to "be strong in the Lord and in the power of His might" (Eph. 6:10). For us to be strong, God must strengthen us. This is accomplished in Christ.

If we try to "be strong" in our own strength, we fall victim to the devil's tactic of pride. But since we can be strengthened "in the Lord," we can have both humility and victory.

Life is a war against a spiritual enemy we cannot see. We can't win on our own, but the God who sees all gives us a courage, perseverance, and wisdom to win an otherwise unwinnable war in Christ.

Do you feel weary today from life's battles? Rest in Christ. Your victory is assured.

Read *James 4:6–8.*

Whom does God oppose and whom does he help? *(God opposes the proud, but he gives grace to the humble.)*

How do we resist the devil? *(By submitting to and drawing near to God.)*

When you sense you're "under attack," do you try to defend yourself and attack the problem in your own strength or in the strength of God?

Prayer

Thank Jesus that he has been victorious over Satan and that in him you are strengthened to fight the fight against him. Express your trust in his strength to fight this battle.

DAY 6

In *The Lion, the Witch and the Wardrobe*, four children enter the magical land of Narnia through a wardrobe. Soon they discover that it was foretold that the four of them would defeat the evil White Witch and deliver Narnia from a seemingly endless winter.

To prepare them for the battles that lie ahead of them, Father Christmas provides the children with weapons. In the same way we have been provided weapons in our battle against Satan. But unlike the weapons in this fictional book, our weapons are real and spiritual.

Paul wrote of these weapons in Ephesians.

Some of our weapons are offensive, for the forward progress of the kingdom of God through the gospel and church of Jesus Christ. Others are defensive; they are meant to protect us from our enemy and his attacks on us.

Jesus doesn't leave us to our own strategies to fight this war. He leads the charge through his defeat of Satan, sin, and death and equips us with powerful weapons.

Read *2 Corinthians 10:4; Ephesians 6:13–20.*

What are the weapons that God has given us for battle against our enemy? *(The belt of truth, the breastplate of righteousness, gospel shoes, the shield of faith, the helmet of salvation, the sword of the Spirit (Scripture), prayer, and the ability to stand.)*

Do you readily use these weapons in battle?

How can you better employ this arsenal?

Prayer

Pray, "Lord Jesus Christ, I ask that you send any demons and evil spirits away from me. Devil, in the name and authority of Jesus, I command you to get away from me and my family."

DAY 7

Life is war. There's no doubt about it. The only question that needs to be answered is, "Which side are you on?"

In Adam, a war was lost. In Jesus, a war was won. Satan tempted our first parents to sin, and they did. Their one act of disobedience involved us all in their tragedy and misery. This means that we're all born sinners by nature and live as sinners by choice.

As a Christian, you were once a captive in this war until Jesus offered you grace and peace with him. If you are in Christ, then you are at peace with God and have been empowered by his grace to victoriously live out your new identity in Christ.

In Christ you are forgiven; you are clean. Your captivity has been replaced with a new identity. But if you are not in Christ, then this life is the closest to heaven that you'll ever get.

If you are in Christ, then this life is the closest to hell you'll ever get. So as Winston Churchill once said, "If you're going through hell, keep going."

Read *Colossians 2:13–15.*

What did God do with our record of sin debt in Christ? *(He canceled it and set our sin aside by nailing it to the cross.)*

What did Jesus' death on our behalf do to the devil and demonic forces? *(It disarmed the rulers and authorities and put them to open shame by triumphing over them.)*

Illustrate this with your family by having everyone write down their sins on paper and nailing them to a board.

Prayer

Thank Jesus that he took the record of your sin debt and nailed it to the cross, paying the penalty that you deserved.

FOOTNOTES

1. Patrick Stump, "We Liked You Better Fat: Confessions of a Pariah" (entry, Patrick Stump blog), February 28, 2012, http://www.patrickstump.com/.

2. J. Todd Billings, *Union with Christ: Reframing Theology and Ministry for the Church* (Grand Rapids: Baker Academic, 2011), 16.

3. Crossway Books, 2005

4. Patrick Stump, "We Liked You Better Fat: Confessions of a Pariah" (entry, Patrick Stump blog), February 28, 2012, http://www.patrickstump.com/.

5. J. Todd Billings, *Union with Christ: Reframing Theology and Ministry for the Church* (Grand Rapids: Baker Academic, 2011), 16.

6. Crossway Books, 2005

SMALL GROUP STUDY

HOW TO USE THIS STUDY

This study has been designed to help your small group discover the transforming power of having an identity grounded in Jesus Christ. Use this guide for note keeping and to journal along the way.

FIRST AND FOREMOST, THE GOSPEL: The good news that Jesus saves sinners is foundational to this study. In response to the good news of God's gift of free grace, Christians gladly submit to God and his Word. Because Christians can be sure of God's loving-kindness, submission to God (while not always easy) is joyful, and in the process of joyful submission, we are changed.

GROUP GATHERINGS: Before you meet as a group, take some time to review the introduction and reacquaint yourself with the content in order to prepare for the discussion. Begin each session by watching a short video and/or reading a scripture reflection. Questions are provided for each week to help your group dig deep into the topics.

PRAYER: It's common for a group to leave little time for prayer, but be encouraged to make this priority.

EXPERIENCE: The last section for each week explains the small group experience times, and each experience is designed to reinforce what the group is learning together about identity in Jesus. Many of the experience times will be done as a group; others can be completed alone. Some experiences require preplanning, so be sure to look ahead and make the arrangements accordingly.

SAFETY: What does it mean to "be safe" as you share details about your personal life? The content of this study is personal, so talk openly about what safety means for your group.

WHAT *SAFE* MEANS:

1. Lead with grace.

2. Listen before giving advice.

3. Group participants are free to wrestle with ideas and even disagree without judgment, personal attack, or dismissal.

4. Don't gossip, not even through prayer.

WHAT *SAFE* DOES NOT MEAN:

1. *Safe* does not mean we are safe to sin: community should be a dangerous place for sin as we call one another to confession and repentance.

2. *Safe* does not mean that we avoid participation: Community is not a safe place to hide. It is a safe place to live out God's call on our lives.

Be committed to foster safety in your group together, as you're challenged and sanctified by the Word of God. If you don't feel safe in your group, tell your leader. If your *leader* is the source of your concern, please let a pastor know so he can help.

As you work through this study guide, and discover that you haven't accepted the gift of God's free grace, be encouraged to speak with your group leader or a pastor and become a Christian today!

SMALL GROUP STUDY

INTRODUCTION

Where do you get your worth?

If you can answer that question, you will know how you define your identity and your values, and how that guides your decision making. Therefore, embracing your identity in Christ is essential to the Christian life.

Biblically, individuals aren't the only ones who receive new identities; we have received a new corporate identity. To be made new in Christ means to be part of his people. So we don't take this journey alone, but walk and wrestle through our sin, God's word to us, and its implications.

The implications of how an identity is derived are huge. Identity dictates how we interact with the rest of the world, and that includes what we worship, as well as our mission in life. When identity flows from a life with Jesus, manifested in worship of Him, community in the church and empowered mission for the sake of the gospel.

If you are a Christian, you were changed the moment you came to faith in Christ. Unfortunately, many Christians fail to live in light of that identity and end up settling for much less. As you work through this study over the next sixteen weeks, my prayer for you and your community is that you will joyfully embrace your identity in Jesus and walk boldly in Christ to the glory of God.

WEEK 1

I AM _____?

INTRODUCTION: _Read!_

Who do you think you are?

Our world bombards us with so many competing things and ideas that sometimes it's hard to answer the question. It seems as if somebody else is dead set on defining you, or bullying you into defining yourself, by the shoes you wear, the soda you drink, and the music you listen to on your smartphone. Yes, even your smartphone can be a source of your identity.

Yet even more telling is the foundation of the question. Who do you _think_ you are?

What if you could _know_ who you are? How would that change the equation?

This week we begin a sixteen-week study on who we _really_ are. We call this our _identity_. And because of the person and work of Jesus Christ, we don't have to guess when we answer this question. Our goal by the end of this study is for each of us to be walking boldly in the truth of our identity rooted in Christ.

This week, however, we will start at the beginning: understanding where we are today as individuals and as a community.

What is the true source of your identity when your foundation is shaken by tragedy or windfall? Truth be told, because we rarely consider from where we've received our identity, we're unable to see the profound impact identity has on every decision we make and on how we see the world. But as we take the time to consider such questions, we begin to give room for the Holy Spirit to remind us of the one from whom our identity comes.

So this week we start with a simple question: Who do _you_ think you are?

VIDEO RESPONSE:

How would you describe yourself to someone you just met?

What clues point to where derive worth? How common to state vocation? How does this inform about how we think of identity? By WHAT we do rather than what believe.

133

my identity is given to me, NOT acheived by me.

SMALL GROUP STUDY

SCRIPTURE READING:

Genesis 1:26–27:

Then God said, "Let us make man in our image, after our likeness. And let them have dominion over the fish of the sea and over the birds of the heavens and over the livestock and over all the earth and over every creeping thing that creeps on the earth.

So God created man in his own image,
in the image of God he created him;
male and female he created them.

GROUP QUESTIONS:

1. How does your perceived identity affect your everyday life? Give some examples.

2. From what are you prone to get your identity, other than Jesus? (Items, duties, others, longings, sufferings?)

3. What does being made in the image of God mean to you?

4. What is an image bearer? How do we practically image God?

5. Think of a time of crisis in your life. Did you discover anything about finding your identity in something or someone other than Jesus through that experience?

6. Why is it important for you to personally understand who you are?

PRAYER:

- As we explore where we are finding our identity, let us pray for God to reveal even the secret places from which we try to get our identity, so we can root them out and lay them before the cross.

- Pray for the Holy Spirit to give us strength to speak truth to one another even when it is difficult, and the courage to hear truth.

- Lastly, pray for those we know who have never trusted in Jesus as their Savior and who are crippled by an identity in something other than him. Pray that God will use our community to bring the good news to them.

EXPERIENCE:

This week we are going to do a little recon on the assault on our identity. Get a notebook that will fit into your pocket or use your favorite electronic device, and keep it ready.

During the week, choose a magazine, a TV show, and a social media site that you frequent most. While you're enjoying these forms of media, answer the following questions:

Magazine:

Name of the magazine:
Theme of the magazine:

As you read each article, look for where the writer wants you to find your identity. Make a list by article of each source of identity.

What do the various writers offer you if you put your identity in these things?

Do the same for each ad.

Show:

Name of the show:
Theme of the show:

As you watch the show, make a list of each character and where you suspect each one finds his or her identity. What do the characters value? What would they die for? What makes them feel alive?

What is the moral or agenda of the show? (In other words, what did the show want you to learn or leave with when it finished?) How does identity play into the show's agenda?

For each commercial answer the following questions:

What was the commercial promoting?
In what did its sponsor want you to find your identity?
What did the commercial offer/promise you ?

Social Media:

Name of the website:

As you read the various posts, list each one that may offer a clue to where the user finds his or her identity (leave out names):

How does social media site use identity?

What are the most common areas of identity that you see as you peruse the site?

WEEK 2
I AM IN CHRIST

INTRODUCTION:

I am in Christ.

This changes everything.

Such a simple truth: I am in Christ. But this sends a shock wave through the jumbled mess of false identity and rips through all the noise and chatter. Being in Christ reigns as judge over notions of peer pressure and status and brings clarity in the fog.

This week we'll meditate on what it means to be "in Christ—the only bedrock on which we can and must build our identity. An identity rooted in anything else is empty of promise and leads to destruction and death, joy that does not sustain, and fulfillment that is never realized.

But as we study what Ephesians says about identity in Christ, our goal is to see the wonderful freedom found in fully understanding and believing in faith the truth of our identity in Christ. This will give us the power to overcome idolatry in our lives and to live fully devoted to our Lord and Savior, Jesus.

READING RESPONSE:

Think of a time when you had a significant change in your life (graduated from school, changed jobs, lost a job, got promoted. etc.); describe how a new title or role in life changed how you saw yourself.

REVIEW:

Spend some time at the beginning of your time together this week reviewing your experiences from last week. Share what you learned about identity as you watched TV, read magazines, and surfed the web. What was the most surprising to you as you intentionally looked for issues of identity in your daily life?

SMALL GROUP STUDY

SCRIPTURE READING:

Ephesians 1:1–14:

Paul, an apostle of Christ Jesus by the will of God,
  To the saints who are in Ephesus, and are faithful in Christ Jesus:
  Grace to you and peace from God our Father and the Lord Jesus Christ.

SPIRITUAL BLESSINGS IN CHRIST

Blessed be the God and Father of our Lord Jesus Christ, who has blessed us in Christ with every spiritual blessing in the heavenly places, even as he chose us in him before the foundation of the world, that we should be holy and blameless before him. In love he predestined us for adoption as sons through Jesus Christ, according to the purpose of his will, to the praise of his glorious grace, with which he has blessed us in the Beloved. In him we have redemption through his blood, the forgiveness of our trespasses, according to the riches of his grace, which he lavished upon us, in all wisdom and insight making known to us the mystery of his will, according to his purpose, which he set forth in Christ as a plan for the fullness of time, to unite all things in him, things in heaven and things on earth.

In him we have obtained an inheritance, having been predestined according to the purpose of him who works all things according to the counsel of his will, so that we who were the first to hope in Christ might be to the praise of his glory. In him you also, when you heard the word of truth, the gospel of your salvation, and believed in him, were sealed with the promised Holy Spirit, who is the guarantee of our inheritance until we acquire possession of it, to the praise of his glory. (ESV)

GROUP QUESTIONS:

1. What is the difference between biography and testimony? *present,*
2. What does it mean for a person to be "in" something? *belong, be a part of*
3. How many times did Paul refer to being "in Christ" in the first fourteen verses of Ephesians 1? What does it mean to you to be "in Christ"?

4. How does understanding your identity in Christ help you battle the false identities we looked at last week in the homework?

PRAYER:

- Thank Jesus for bringing us into himself. Share with him what it means that you are in him.

- Pray for the Holy Spirit to continue in the work of opening our eyes to the things in our lives that are competing for our source of identity.

- Pray for those we know who are not yet in Christ, that they will soon find their identity in him who saves.

EXPERIENCE:

This week we will each construct two outlines of our lives, from two points of view.

First, outline the significant moments in your life, in the style of a biography. Think of how you would tell your life story with the perspective that you are the central figure. You don't have to write out the complete story; just make an outline of key moments.

Second, outline the significant moments in your life from the perspective of a testimony to God. What does this outline look like with the point of view that God is the central figure?

Biography   Testimony

Once you have finished, reflect on how the perspective (biography versus testimony) affects how you experience each event in your life:

WEEK 3
I AM A SAINT

INTRODUCTION:

Very few of us dare to introduce ourselves as saints. In our culture, such a salutation would be considered out of place and arrogant. Two issues come to mind.

First, we don't understand what it means to be a saint. Culturally, the term *saint* is borrowed predominantly from the Catholic notion of sainthood, mixed with comic book ideals, self-actualization, and karma. All these elements blend together and give a picture of a person rising above the rest to accomplish extraordinary, selfless acts. While not necessarily sinless, saints are a cut above the average moral fiber of society. In the Catholic tradition a saint must meet specific qualifications, which include performing miracles in life and/or death. Such definitions have the effect of making sainthood feel out of reach for most of us and reserved for the best.

The second issue of sainthood is related to having clarity of our own sin. A man once told me that it doesn't matter how good a soup you are eating once a fly lands in it. No matter how good that soup was, all you can see is that fly. Now, it is important for us to understand the depth and extent of depravity within our lives. This is because it is a vital reminder of our need for a Savior. But it's also equally important to remember that on this side of the cross we are made new in Christ. When we find our identity in being a sinner, it becomes increasingly easier to justify sin and become acclimated to it in our lives.

Both of these issues are man-focused. The first puts sainthood on your shoulders as if you can earn it, and the second puts it on your shoulders as if you can lose it.

The truth is, we're made saints through the life, death, and resurrection of Jesus. He did the work to make us saints, and therefore we can neither earn nor lose our identity as saints.

VIDEO RESPONSE:

What images do you think of when you hear someone called a saint?

REVIEW:

Have people share what they learned by comparing their biographies with their testimonies. Discuss how the perspective of God at the center of our stories changed the way we view major events in our lives.

SCRIPTURE READING:

Ephesians 1:1–2:

> Paul, an apostle of Christ Jesus by the will of God, to the saints who are in Ephesus, and are faithful in Christ Jesus: Grace to you and peace from God our Father and the Lord Jesus Christ." (ESV)

GROUP QUESTIONS:

1. Do you more readily identify yourself as a sinner or a saint? Explain why.

2. What difference would it make in your day-to-day life to identify as a saint? *Assurance, confidence (in salvation)*

3. Why is it important to you that sin does not remove the image of God in us?

4. How does that affect the way we treat one another?

5. How does that affect the way we treat sinners who have not been saved by Jesus?

6. Discuss the meaning and importance of the following:
   a. Justification — *"accepted by God"*
   b. Sanctification — *journey to becoming Christlike*
   c. Glorification — *"are Christlike in heaven"*

7. How does our identity free us from the obligation to sin? *no longer a slave to sin. we are free, no longer obliged to. master of sin*

8. What does grief over sin look like in your life?

9. As saints, how can we help one another pursue humility?

PRAYER:

- Thank Jesus for making it possible for us to be reckoned as saints through his life, death, and resurrection.

- Pray for the Holy Spirit to continue the work of sanctification in us as we walk in our identity as saints.

- Pray that we will remain faithful until the day we see Jesus in his full glory.

EXPERIENCE:

Ephesians 1 reminds us of the blessings we have received through the perfect life, death, and resurrection of Jesus. This week our homework will look forward to the next session (I Am Blessed).

Spend some time in prayer, and make a list of all the ways in which you feel you have been blessed. Bring the list next week, and be ready to discuss.

Saint —
greek word origins
latin → "sanctus"

Big Idea: Christians don't have to manipulate God to be blessed.

WEEK 4
I AM BLESSED

INTRODUCTION:

Have you ever bought someone lunch just to treat him? He didn't earn it, and you weren't paying him back . . . you just wanted to bless him?

As a dad, this is my favorite thing to do for my kids. I love to surprise them with a gift or with a time out together that they didn't see coming and didn't ask for. I do this because I love my children.

This is how God blesses us. We did not ask for it, nor did we earn it. Quite the contrary, actually, yet he has blessed us and continues to bless us. He does so because he loves us.

Unfortunately, we have a predisposition toward a works-based theology. All that means is that ~~we prefer to earn love rather than receive it for free~~. This is why so many wrestle with the gospel. It cannot be won. But the more we know God, the better this news becomes as we realize we could never earn God's love through our tainted works. We must therefore rely on his love and grace. And while it can be difficult to relinquish our grip on working for God's approval, once we do, it is the most freeing moment in our lives.

Instead of working so hard to appease God or manipulate him into blessing us, we can spend our time praising him for his grace in our lives. As we understand how much we have been blessed by God, we begin to appreciate his love in new ways and are drawn to worship him with our lives.

READING RESPONSE:

~~How would you define a blessing?~~ *count your blessings question . . .*

REVIEW:

Take out your list from last week's Experience and discuss how many things on your list are self-focused versus God-focused. In other words, what things on your list required the death and resurrection of Jesus (and are eternal blessings), and which are merely temporal or circumstantial? For help, compare them to the list of blessings in chapter 4: holiness, predestination, adoption, redemption, forgiveness, grace, and being sealed. What does this reveal about our perception of blessing (now or eternal)?

SCRIPTURE READING:

Ephesians 1:3–14:

Blessed be the God and Father of our Lord Jesus Christ, who has blessed us with every spiritual blessing in the heavenly *places* in Christ, *just as He chose us in Him before the foundation of the world, that we should be holy and without blame before Him in love, having predestined us to adoption as sons by Jesus Christ to Himself, according to the good pleasure of His will, to the praise of the glory of His grace, by which He made us accepted in the Beloved. In Him we have redemption through His blood, the forgiveness of sins, according to the riches of His grace which He made to abound toward us in all wisdom and prudence, having made known to us the mystery of His will, according to His good pleasure which He purposed in Himself, that in the dispensation of the fullness of the times He might gather together in one all things in Christ, both which are in heaven and which are on earth—in Him. In Him also we have obtained an inheritance, being predestined according to the purpose of Him who works all things according to the counsel of His will, that we who first trusted in Christ should be to the praise of His glory. In Him you also trusted, after you heard the word of truth, the gospel of your salvation; in whom also, having believed, you were sealed with the Holy Spirit of promise, who is the guarantee of our inheritance until the redemption of the purchased possession, to the praise of His glory.*

GROUP QUESTIONS:

Focus: How our identity in christ relates to the blessings of God.

1. Have you ever tried to manipulate God into blessing you? How?

2. In what ways does an identity in Christ free Christians from trying to manipulate God?

3. In what ways have you been blessed by God?

salvation = ultimate blessing!

*God blesses his children b/c He loves them.
blessing is not simply material or circumstantial.
christians are most blessed through receiving a
new identity in Jesus.*

146

A focus on temporal & circumstantial blessing can lead to crisis of faith in times of trial.

4. Why is it important to think of the eternal blessing of God rather then mere circumstances or temporal blessings?

5. We are a blessed people. What do our blessings reveal about the character of God? (Consider Genesis 1:26.) *God wants to make Himself known.*

6. Why does God bless us?

7. How does being blessed by God affect how we bless others?

PRAYER:

- Thank God for the generosity he has shown us in the way he blesses us.

- Pray that we will see opportunities to bless one another.

- Pray that we will be given opportunities to bless our neighbors and show them the kindness of Jesus.

EXPERIENCE:

We have been looking, in Ephesians 1, at how we have been blessed. This week your goal is to bless others. We call this experience "Bless a Stranger."

As a community, pick a morning or afternoon when you can gather at your favorite coffee or pastry shop. Have everyone contribute to a gift card so you will have a significant amount of money collected. Present the card to the cashier and inform her that you will be covering the next customers in line until the gift card runs out. Find a place to sit, and discuss what you enjoy and what you find hard about blessing complete strangers.

- Does your satisfaction change based on whether you are thanked or not?

- Is it harder or easier to bless a stranger than someone you know? Why?

- Was it difficult to contribute money to blessing a stranger?

- What reactions surprised you the most as you watched people receive free coffee or doughnuts?

- Lastly, think through and journal about how this experience helped you understand the character of God in deeper way.

As an alternative, do this exercise on your own by picking someone to bless. But there are some rules:

1. This cannot involve paying someone back who has done you a recent kindness.

2. The person you bless cannot be someone who can benefit you.

3. You should not expect repayment.

When you find the person you want to bless, do it in a way that is appropriate (buy him lunch, pick up her favorite coffee, mow his or her lawn, etc.).

After you have completed the exercise, journal about how it made you feel to bless someone just to be a blessing. Did you have trouble finding someone without having a motive? Was it difficult to bless someone because you didn't have it in your budget? Did the person's gratitude affect your joy in blessing her or him? Did you like it?

Finally, think through and journal about how this experience helped you understand the character of God in deeper way.

Recognize — understand full [worth] of

WEEK 5 VALUE

I AM APPRECIATED

— recognize full worth of
— understand fully

INTRODUCTION:

Our culture presents a thousand things to preoccupy our minds and fill us
with anxiety. We're always so busy we can barely take a breath. In such a
fast-paced world, it can seem as though we are drowning in decisions and
circumstances. It can also feel very lonely.

As we fight to remain faithful to the work Christ has done in us among
the other battles of life (relationships, work, school, health, and so forth), it
can feel as if God does not see us in our struggles. Certainly this is a poor
understanding of God, but that does not make it feel any less real.

So it's comforting that Paul took the time to remind the Ephesians that
he had heard of their good works and that he was praying for them. These
are simple words that remind us that God is with us always. He sees the small
victories in our lives as we turn from sin and run from temptation. Even when
we fail and we turn back to him in confession and repentance, He is there to
comfort us and remind us that we are seen.

So take heart this week as we look at the prayer Paul prayed for the Ephesians and us, and recognize that God is with you and that you are significant
in the family of God.

VIDEO RESPONSE:

Who are the people you most appreciate in your life?

REVIEW:

Discuss your experience from last week. As you reflected on blessing others
without condition, how did that open your eyes to the generosity of God?

engages me, not just me them

SMALL GROUP STUDY

SCRIPTURE READING:

talking or peer (not better)

Ephesians 1:15–23:

A

Therefore I also, after I heard of your faith in the Lord Jesus and your love for all the saints, do not cease to give thanks for you, making mention of you in my prayers; that the God of our Lord Jesus Christ, the Father of glory, may give to you the spirit of wisdom and revelation in the knowledge of Him, the eyes of your understanding being enlightened; that you may know what is the hope of His calling, what are the riches of the glory of His inheritance in the saints, and what is the exceeding greatness of His power toward us who believe, according to the working of His mighty power which He worked in Christ when He raised Him from the dead and seated Him at His right hand in the heavenly places, far above all principality and power and might and dominion, and every name that is named, not only in this age but also in that which is to come. And He put all things under His feet, and gave Him to be head over all things to the church, which is His body, the fullness of Him who fills all in all.

B

GROUP QUESTIONS:

1. How does being appreciated by a boss, parent, or other person in authority affect you personally?

2. What does it mean to you that God sees and appreciates your faithfulness even when others do not?

3. Looking at the chart below, do you ever find yourself on the unappreciated side? How does having our identity rooted in Christ move us from the left to the right?

UNAPPRECIATED	APPRECIATED
Grumbling	Praying A
Competing	Celebrating
Bitterness	Thanksgiving B
Performing	Serving
Boasting	Encouraging

150 *affection – abuse*
encouraging – discouraging

4. Who in your life do you appreciate the most? Explain why.

5. Do you feel you have experienced the understanding of the things Paul prayed for us in Ephesians 1:15–23?

6. What image of Jesus do you get from these verses?

7. How does that magnify the idea that He sees and appreciates our faithfulness?

8. In what ways does an accurate picture of the majesty of Jesus reduce our need to be appreciated?

PRAYER:

- Pray through Ephesians 5:1–23 for one another, using Paul's words simply as a guide as you tailor your prayer to your group members.

- Pray that our view of Jesus will continue to grow and lead to worship of him alone.

- Pray that we will be content with the appreciation of our Lord rather than let our happiness be determined by others.

EXPERIENCE: *show appreciation on other's terms*

Paul encouraged us in Ephesians 1:15–23 as he reminded us that God sees our faithfulness. This week our experience will be more individual as we each write a letter of encouragement to someone we appreciate. Pray through who the Lord might place on your heart who could use a word of appreciation for his or her faithfulness to Jesus.

Spend some time writing a letter to the individual you chose, to share your appreciation for him or her and to encourage that person. If possible, make it a handwritten letter, but you can also send an e-mail or even a card if time is short.

— putting down phone when talking to

WEEK 6
I AM SAVED

INTRODUCTION:

If you have never dangled two hundred feet in the air over the edge of a cliff, you probably don't have as much appreciation for the tensile strength of a ten-millimeter rope as a climber who just lost his footing.

The joy of salvation is most acute when we are faced with the prospect of destruction. New Christians can attest to this fact. Yet whether we are new Christians or have walked with Jesus for decades, it is always important for us to remember that our identity in Christ was attained when we were pulled from the path of God's wrath. We were made alive in Christ even though we were dead and headed for destruction.

This work of salvation was the singular work of Jesus, as it says in Ephesians 2:9, "*For by grace you have been saved through faith, and that not of yourselves; it is* the gift of God, not of works, lest anyone should boast."

This truth should have lasting implication in the way we live our lives and experience God. Our response to Jesus in worship and good works will grow as we are reminded of what we have been saved from, by whom we have been saved, and for what we have been saved.

You are saved by Jesus to glorify God through the good works he's prepared for you. Infuse each moment of your day with the grace shown to you by Christ. There is nothing more powerful in this world than a Christian rightly understanding the grace of God and applying that grace in all facets of life. By doing so, we show Christ to our spouses, our children, our friends, our family, our coworkers—even our enemies—that many may be saved. (chap. 6)

READING RESPONSE:

Have someone share a time when he or she was saved from eminent danger. Ask the speaker to describe the emotion (s)he felt when (s)he realized (s)he was safe.

153

[handwritten: Big Idea: Being saved by Jesus has a lasting implication in the way Christians live their lives & experience.]

REVIEW:

Discuss how you felt writing a letter of appreciation to someone last week. How did this experience help you understand the appreciation that God has for you in the letter he wrote to you through Ephesians?

SCRIPTURE READING:

Ephesians 2:1–10:

And you He made alive, who were dead in trespasses and sins, in which you once walked according to the course of this world, according to the prince of the power of the air, the spirit who now works in the sons of disobedience, among whom also we all once conducted ourselves in the lusts of our flesh, fulfilling the desires of the flesh and of the mind, and were by nature children of wrath, just as the others.

But God, who is rich in mercy, because of His great love with which He loved us, even when we were dead in trespasses, made us alive together with Christ (by grace you have been saved), and raised us up together, and made us sit together in the heavenly places in Christ Jesus, that in the ages to come He might show the exceeding riches of His grace in His kindness toward us in Christ Jesus. For by grace you have been saved through faith, and that not of yourselves; it is the gift of God, not of works, lest anyone should boast. For we are His workmanship, created in Christ Jesus for good works, which God prepared beforehand that we should walk in them.

[handwritten margin: merciful LOVING KIND]

GROUP QUESTIONS:

1. Discuss the importance of being saved, with respect to the past, the present, and the future.

2. From what are we saved in each of those three contexts?

3. Which of these three is the easiest for you to relate to, and which is the hardest?

4. For what are we being saved? *[handwritten: Worship & good works with deeper knowledge of Jesus person & work.]*

5. In what ways does Jesus receive glory through saving his people?

6. How are good works a result of being saved?

7. What does Ephesians 2:1–10 tell us about the character of God?

PRAYER:

- Thank God for saving us while we were still in rebellion against him.

- Pray that we will help one another grow in faithfulness and holiness as we are sanctified in Christ.

- Pray that the Holy Spirit will help us be faithful to the good works for which he has prepared us.

EXPERIENCE:

Ephesians 2 reminds us that we were once children of wrath and that Jesus has saved us, making us new in him. For your experience this week, read through Ephesians 2:1–10 and pray through the sins you committed before coming to Christ, as well as those sins with which you continue to struggle. Write these sins on a piece of paper, along with the source of identity that leads to them and the outcome to which such sins will lead. On a separate sheet of paper, make a list of the promises you receive in Christ from Ephesians.

Now take the first list and destroy it just as Jesus destroyed the sin nature in us on the cross. Bury it in the yard, burn it in the grill or in a bonfire, or shred it in a shredder. Then pray through the list of promises and thank God for saving you from destruction.

Saved from:
Past sin.
Present sin
Future sin

5 ways God showed me kindness this week

---

1) through beauty of His creation

2) through laughter w/ sisters

3) through providence for my family w/ cabin - so generous.

4) through friends (Hough/Lehmann's) that regard me as family.

5) through showing me what contentment is.

WEEK 7
I AM RECONCILED

INTRODUCTION:

First Peter 2:10 says that "once [we] were not a people" in reference to our lives before Jesus (ESV). We are reminded that before we were given a new identity in Christ, we stood in rebellion against the God of the universe. Because sin separates, that enmity also extends beyond God into all of our relationships and separates what God has brought together.

This verse highlights the significance of the reconciling power of the cross. Jesus, through his perfect life, death on the cross, and resurrection, removed the enmity that existed between God and his people. Jesus reconciled us to God and to one another.

Now we are agents of reconciliation in the world, for Jesus reconciled us while we were still in rebellion against him. It's not that he waited until we relented. No, he pursued reconciliation for us without our help.

Being recipients of such grace gives us a new identity to work that empowers and motivates us to extend such an effort to others.

VIDEO RESPONSE:

Describe times when you have seen reconciliation take place in your life. What were some significant moments that defined reconciliation for you?

REVIEW:

Share what you learned about your identity as you went through the ceremony last week of putting your old nature to death through Jesus. How did that affect your appreciation for the saving power of the cross?

Big Idea: Those who have been reconciled to God in Christ are able to make reconciliation with others.

SCRIPTURE READING:

Ephesians 2:11–22:

Therefore remember that you, once Gentiles in the flesh—who are called Uncircumcision by what is called the Circumcision made in the flesh by hands—that at that time you were without Christ, being aliens from the commonwealth of Israel and strangers from the covenants of promise, having no hope and without God in the world. But now in Christ Jesus you who once were far off have been brought near by the blood of Christ. For He Himself is our peace, who has made both one, and has broken down the middle wall of separation, having abolished in His flesh the enmity, that is, the law of commandments *contained* in ordinances, *so as to create in Himself one new man from the two, thus* making peace, *and that He might reconcile them both to God in one body through the cross, thereby putting to death the enmity.* And He came and preached peace to you who were afar off and to those who were near. For through Him we both have access by one Spirit to the Father. Now, therefore, you are no longer strangers and foreigners, but fellow citizens with the saints and members of the household of God, having been built on the foundation of the apostles and prophets, Jesus Christ Himself being the chief cornerstone, *in whom the whole building, being fitted together, grows into a holy temple in the Lord, in whom you also are being built together for a dwelling place of God in the Spirit.*

reconciliation btwn Jews/Gentiles = picture of how cross has reconciled us to God and one another

GROUP QUESTIONS:

1. How does Jesus provide the antidote to human division? unification in him

2. In what ways is Jesus your peace in the midst of conflict?

3. How have you personally experienced division?

4. How does our identity pave the way for reconciliation?

5. Many of us take pride in our cultural tribe or heritage. In what ways do you struggle with letting Jesus be your primary identity?

6. How have you experienced reconciliation with God?

7. How have you experienced that reconciliation between you and others?

PRAYER:

- Thank Jesus for providing a way for peace and reconciling us to God.
- Pray for reconciliation within our community if there is any conflict or enmity between our members.
- Pray that the Holy Spirit will show us where we can be agents of reconciliation within our neighborhood.

EXPERIENCE:

Ephesians 2:11–22 shows us that in and through Christ we can be empowered as agents of reconciliation. For our experience this week, we are going to throw a neighborhood barbecue. Put together a plan for a great party that will be fun and comfortable for your neighbors. Consider having it at the local community center or a park if that would make it less intimidating. Plan on having good food and activities for the kids. The goal of the barbecue is to be hospitable to our neighbors and bring the neighborhood together in light of the reconciling work of Jesus.

- What does it mean to be ambassadors of reconciliation within our small group as well as within the world?
- Identity in Jesus leads to confidence in approaching God.
- Hesitancy to receive reconciliation is an indication of an identity distortion.

WEEK 8
I AM AFFLICTED

INTRODUCTION:

Nobody wants to face pain and heartache in life. It would be morbid to desire such things. But that doesn't mean affliction should be avoided.

We've been given a new identity in Christ, but we still live in a world affected by sin. This will be the case until Jesus returns in glory to judge the world and complete his redemptive plan.

Until then all mankind will suffer various degrees of affliction. Those of us in Christ should expect it all the more, as we'll likely suffer like Jesus and for Jesus. The first half of Ephesians 3 suggests as much, as Paul described his tribulation as part and parcel of his opportunity to preach the gospel to nonbelievers.

How grateful we should be that Paul didn't give up in the face of hardship for the cause of the gospel, since we are the product of his faithfulness.

This week, as we discuss what it means to face affliction as a believer, continue to think of the legacy your faithfulness will affect. Who will look back in hundreds of years and be thankful that you did not wilt in the face of affliction?

So be encouraged:

One day, we will see Christ face-to-face. Our faith will be sight. His nail-scarred hands will wipe our tears away. All who are in Christ will sing his praises and see his glory together forever. He will work out all things for the good of those who love him. All our questions will be answered, our hopes will be realized, and our fears will be forgotten. Until that day, we will be afflicted, but our identity in Christ need not be affected. (chap. 8)

VIDEO RESPONSE:

How would you define *affliction*?

REVIEW:

Discuss your experience from last week's barbecue. Most of us associate with others based on affinity and mutual affection. But everybody has a quirky neighbor. Some of us even have neighbors we'd prefer to avoid. Consider that the issues we have with others aren't always even issues of sin preferences but simply annoyances. Now, think about how God in Christ reconciled us even amid our sin! In light of all this, what did you learn about the power of the gospel when it comes to being agents of reconciliation? Is there any reason you would withhold the gospel from a neighbor? Why?

SCRIPTURE READING:

Ephesians 3:1–13:

For this reason I, Paul, the prisoner of Christ Jesus for you Gentiles—if indeed you have heard of the dispensation of the grace of God which was given to me for you, how that by revelation He made known to me the mystery (as I have briefly written already, by which, when you read, you may understand my knowledge in the mystery of Christ), which in other ages was not made known to the sons of men, as it has now been revealed by the Spirit to His holy apostles and prophets: that the Gentiles should be fellow heirs, of the same body, and partakers of His promise in Christ through the gospel, of which I became a minister according to the gift of the grace of God given to me by the effective working of His power. To me, who am less than the least of all the saints, this grace was given, that I should preach among the Gentiles the unsearchable riches of Christ, and to make all see what is the fellowship of the mystery, which from the beginning of the ages has been hidden in God who created all things through Jesus Christ; to the intent that now the manifold wisdom of God might be made known by the church to the principalities and powers in the heavenly places, according to the eternal purpose which He accomplished in Christ Jesus our Lord, in whom we have boldness and access with confidence through faith in Him. Therefore I ask that you do not lose heart at my tribulations for you, which is your glory.

GROUP QUESTIONS:

1. Have you ever felt afflicted? How do we discern whether or not affliction is related to our faith in Christ or is a result of our own sin, folly, or general suffering due to the Fall?

2. Do you tend to expect affliction, or do you feel slighted when face it?

3. Why is it important to correctly diagnose affliction when it comes to cause and cure?

4. How can we encourage one another to not lose heart in the face of affliction?

5. When you are suffering, do you tend to ask "why" questions, or "who" questions?

6. "Why" questions can at times undermine the truth that God is good and in control. With what kind of posture are you approaching God when you ask why?

7. How have you been comforted by Jesus during affliction?

8. How did Paul provide us an example of this in Ephesians 3:1–13?

9. In what practical ways can we use our suffering for God's glory?

10. How does our identity in Christ make this possible?

PRAYER:

- Pray that we will ask the right question in the midst of pain in our lives.

- Pray that we will see the compassion of Jesus in the midst of affliction.

- Pray that the Holy Spirit will help us use suffering for the glory of God and the benefit of others.

EXPERIENCE:

In light of Paul's affliction for and because of the gospel, our experience this week will include praying for those who are facing affliction/suffering. Have someone in the group organize a visit to a children's hospital, a sick person in your community, or a nursing home. Feel free to think of an option that has the most meaning to your small group.

Before you go, prepare some care packages or other blessings that would be appropriate. Pray for the Holy Spirit to provide gospel opportunities with those who are hurting.

As you visit, make it your goal to hear the stories of those who are suffering and simply spend time with them. If they are willing, take the time to pray for them.

WEEK 9
I AM HEARD

INTRODUCTION:

I love it when my children come to talk to me. There are few feelings greater than when your child desires to confide in you as a true friend.

We receive many great things when we are made new in Christ, but none as personal as access to the Father through prayer. We are invited to speak openly and honestly with the God of the universe, who created all things but also knows each of us personally and intimately.

Our goal this week is to encourage one another to accept this invitation and cultivate our relationship with God through deep conversation in prayer. Our goal is not to pray better. Prayer is not good or bad so much as it is more or less real. We want to foster honest conversation with God. From the chapter we learned that prayer is:

Personal
Relational
Asking
Yearning
Expecting
Revealing

In this section of Ephesians 3, Paul demonstrated for us the boldness with which we may approach our Father. He provided for us an example of how we need not hedge in our prayers but can bring our requests unfiltered and yet submitted for the glory of Jesus.

The promise is that he is waiting intently for us to confide in him as any child would confide in a loving father. For His glory and His joy as well as yours, accept the invitation.

VIDEO RESPONSE:

What is the difference between hearing and listening?

REVIEW:

Discuss what you learned at your hospital visit last week. It's a simple fact that all of us will suffer physically from natural causes, if not now, then later in life. Although Ephesians 3:1–13 is not a call to the mission to visit the sick and infirm, it is a good reminder that our culture is often unaware of others' suffering. Suffering is something that so often is done out of sight, tucked away from the rest of the world, in a hospital somewhere. Now, consider that Paul's sufferings were not endured because of the general fallenness of the world, but for the sake of the gospel! Paul was doing the will of the Father—and he suffered for it. In light of this, how did your experience change the way you view your own experiences with affliction?

SCRIPTURE READING:

Ephesians 3:14–21

> For this reason I bow my knees to the Father of our Lord Jesus Christ, from whom the whole family in heaven and earth is named, that He would grant you, according to the riches of His glory, to be strengthened with might through His Spirit in the inner man, that Christ may dwell in your hearts through faith; that you, being rooted and grounded in love, may be able to comprehend with all the saints what is the width and length and depth and height—to know the love of Christ which passes knowledge; that you may be filled with all the fullness of God. Now to Him who is able to do exceedingly abundantly above all that we ask or think, according to the power that works in us, to Him be glory in the church by Christ Jesus to all generations, forever and ever. Amen.

GROUP QUESTIONS:

1. How important is it to you that someone takes the time to hear you?

2. How does it make you feel to know that God truly hears you in your prayers?

3. Is that something you easily believe or something you struggle with? Explain why.

4. In the above acronym for PRAYER, which of the attributes resonates most with you, and which resonates least?

5. How does your identity in Christ free you to pray?

6. How does a distorted identity impede prayer?

7. What can we learn from Paul's prayer in Ephesians 3:14–21?

8. What can we do to become a people of prayer within our community?

PRAYER:

• Pray through Ephesians 3:14–21 for one another.

• Use Paul's prayer as a springboard to pray through the PRAYER acronym.

• Pray that we will grow in the authenticity of our prayer with God and that it will become exceedingly real to us as individuals and as a community.

EXPERIENCE:

Because we have received such a great gift in being able to talk to God through prayer, this week we are going to put prayer into practice by going on a prayer walk as a community.

Pick an evening when the group can gather to walk through the neighborhood. You may want to start at someone's home and begin by praying together for the neighborhood and opportunities for gospel conversation to those relationships we are forming within it.

Then set out into the community to pray as you walk. You may do this as one large group or in groups of two or three. You may pray out loud or silently in your head as you walk.

The goal is to pray for your neighbors, their needs and opportunities to build relationships with them, and of course, that they will come to know Jesus.

As you do this, don't miss opportunities! If you see some neighbors, stop and get to know them. This may be the opportunity you were just praying for.

When you are done, gather back at the house to pray through what the Holy Spirit may have laid on your heart during your walk.

WEEK 10
I AM GIFTED

INTRODUCTION:

Paul reminded us in Ephesians 4 that our identity in Christ is part of being called into a body of believers. As such, God has gifted each one of us to benefit the body as well as to fulfill his redemptive mission.

Paul exhorted us to "walk worthy of [our] calling" (v. 1), not neglecting the gifts we have been given, but using them for the benefit of the church and the glory of God.

This week we will spend our time discussing what gifts God has blessed our community with and how we can use our gifts to encourage one another. This is something often neglected within small groups, to our loss. Take the time to recognize the talents and gifts that each member of the community possesses, and then spend some time considering how all of these gifts can be used together to bring glory to Jesus.

"But it should be noted that, while gifts are important, they aren't the most important thing. According to Paul, love is more excellent than all gifts, and those gifts, if not used in love, are worthless.[1] So, we should all the more earnestly pray that God would give us his heart to love and serve the church with those gifts as our 'work of ministry,' just as Jesus did for us" (chap. 10).

READING RESPONSE:

What do you think are your spiritual gifts? How are your gifts being used in serving the church?

REVIEW:

Discuss your impressions from your time last week during your prayer walk. What did you learn about prayer? How did God use that time to bring about conviction regarding our neighbors?

SCRIPTURE READING:

Ephesians 4:1–16

I, therefore, the prisoner of the Lord, beseech you to walk worthy of the calling with which you were called, with all lowliness and gentleness, with longsuffering, bearing with one another in love, endeavoring to keep the unity of the Spirit in the bond of peace. There is one body and one Spirit, just as you were called in one hope of your calling; one Lord, one faith, one baptism; one God and Father of all, who is above all, and through all, and in you all. But to each one of us grace was given according to the measure of Christ's gift. Therefore He says:

> *"When He ascended on high,*
> *He led captivity captive,*
> *And gave gifts to men."*

(Now this, "He ascended"—what does it mean but that He also first descended into the lower parts of the earth? He who descended is also the One who ascended far above all the heavens, that He might fill all things.)

And He Himself gave some to be apostles, some prophets, some evangelists, and some pastors and teachers, for the equipping of the saints for the work of ministry, for the edifying of the body of Christ, till we all come to the unity of the faith and of the knowledge of the Son of God, to a perfect man, to the measure of the stature of the fullness of Christ; that we should no longer be children, tossed to and fro and carried about with every wind of doctrine, by the trickery of men, in the cunning craftiness of deceitful plotting, but, speaking the truth in love, may grow up in all things into Him who is the head—Christ—from whom the whole body, joined and knit together by what every joint supplies, according to the effective working by which every part does its share, causes growth of the body for the edifying of itself in love.

GROUP QUESTIONS:

1. How has God used your natural talents in kingdom work?

2. How can we more effectively exercise our spiritual gifts within our community?

3. How do we keep our spiritual gifts in perspective with the gospel and not make them the ultimate thing?

PRAYER:

- Thank God for blessing us with spiritual gifts for use in building up his church.

- Pray for the Holy Spirit to help us discern our spiritual gifts.

- Pray that the Holy Spirit will help us grow in love for one another so that we use our gifts to edify one another.

EXPERIENCE:

The goal of our experience this week is to continue to discern our spiritual gifts. Begin by asking the following questions and answering them in a journal or in notes:

1. Whom/where do you have a passion to serve?

2. What do you have a burden to do?

3. What needs to you see in the church?

4. What do you find joy in doing for others?

5. What opportunities has God already provided for you to serve others?

6. What things are you best at and have the most success in?

7. What have godly people commended you for doing?

8. What acts of service have given you the deepest sense of satisfaction and joy?

Next, read through the list of gifts in chapter 10 and answer the questions at the end of each section. Put together a list of the top two or three gifts that you think best describe how God has gifted you, and bring it to the group next week. In our review time we will discuss our findings. Oftentimes others will see gifts that we do not see in our own lives. This can be a great way to get confirmation or even challenged on our giftings. Be open to hear what others in the group have to say about your giftings and you may be surprised to learn something new about yourself.

WEEK 11
I AM NEW

INTRODUCTION:

Do you remember playing games with friends when you were a kid? If you didn't like the outcome of a particular play, you could call for a "do over." But life isn't quite like that, is it? A child gives very little consideration to things such as the finality of life.

How many of us as adults wish we could call a "do over"? Consider the compounded weight of sin that is an affront to God and his glory and we're all in desperate need of a fresh start.

This is the beauty of the gospel. As we move from death to life, 2 Corinthians 5:17 says that "if anyone is in Christ, he is a new creation. The old has passed away; behold, the new has come" (ESV).

This is great news! The burden and weight of our sin have been removed. Yet that is not all; we are each given a new heart, set on the things of God, and that means we're not doomed to repeat our mistakes. We can walk in holiness to God, not purely out of obligation, but as a joyful response to his love and kindness. With this in mind, as we struggle in the Christian life, we're reminded of the promise that one day we will go to be with Jesus for eternity, and all that has been tainted by sin will be made new.

This can be summarized in the "effects of Christ's work on the cross for us: justification, regeneration, and glorification. Justification makes us externally new. Regeneration makes us internally new. Glorification makes us eternally new in Christ2" (chap. 11).

VIDEO RESPONSE:

Consider something you have that is new. What are the desirable qualities that you attribute to its newness?

REVIEW:

Have each member of the group present what he or she learned about his/ her giftings during the last week. Take the time to encourage one another when you hear of a gift that is particularly acute in someone or share where you think that individual may be gifted that he or she did not mention. Use this time to encourage one another and help each other discern your spiritual gifts.

SCRIPTURE READING:

Ephesians 4:17–24

This I say, therefore, and testify in the Lord, that you should no longer walk as the rest of the Gentiles walk, in the futility of their mind, having their understanding darkened, being alienated from the life of God, because of the ignorance that is in them, because of the blindness of their heart; who, being past feeling, have given themselves over to lewdness, to work all uncleanness with greediness. But you have not so learned Christ, if indeed you have heard Him and have been taught by Him, as the truth is in Jesus: that you put off, concerning your former conduct, the old man which grows corrupt according to the deceitful lusts, and be renewed in the spirit of your mind, and that you put on the new man which was created according to God, in true righteousness and holiness.

GROUP QUESTIONS:

1. What does it mean to you to be a new creation in Christ?

2. In what ways do you struggle to put off the old self and put on Jesus?

3. How can we as a community help one another live out of our identity as new in Christ?

4. What does it mean to be:
   a) justified?
   b) sanctified?
   c) glorified?

5. We all have default modes of justification that are unbiblical. Which of the four alternative paths of hustification have you tried in the past (assuming you're good enough, self-help spirituality, social causes, or keeping rules)? What was the outcome?

6. In what ways is accepting the grace of God easier and harder?

PRAYER:

- Thank God for making us new.

- Pray that the Holy Spirit will strengthen us to walk in light of being made new in Jesus.

- Pray that God will reveal to us where we seek justification in anything other than him.

EXPERIENCE:

Ephesians 4:17–24 tells us that because we are new creations in Christ, the old man that was at work in each of our hearts has been put to death. This week, in celebration of being made new, we are going to throw a "New"-themed party. We always celebrate newness. We throw bridal showers, weddings, New Year's Day parties, baby showers, etc. Why not throw a party for being made new in Christ!

Be creative, and think through the theme for food and activities. Have a great time, and invite some friends.

WEEK 12
I AM FORGIVEN

INTRODUCTION:

Have you ever seen one of those late-night lawyer commercials? Those ads are proof our world is obsessed with placing blame and bringing responsible parties to justice. Since our culture doesn't accept the possibility of accidents, it's no surprise we're so unfamiliar with forgiveness.

In a world bent on justice, forgiveness of an offense debt or injustice is unheard-of—and has tremendous power.

That Christ removed our debt and calls us forgiven as we continue to add to our debt of sin is scandalous . . . and beautiful. As those who are most aware of our offense and the magnitude of our being forgiven, we are now equipped to walk in that forgiveness with others.

In Ephesians 4 Paul called us to be a people marked by forgiveness. In doing so we shield ourselves from "all bitterness, wrath, anger, clamor, and evil speaking" as well as "all malice" (v. 31).

And we do so because we are forgiven in Christ.

VIDEO RESPONSE:

Do you think we live in a forgiving or unforgiving culture? What do you think attributes to such a culture?

REVIEW:

Discuss how last week's party reinforced your appreciation for the work that Christ accomplished for us on the cross.

SCRIPTURE READING:

Ephesians 4:25–32

Therefore, putting away lying, "Let each one of you speak truth with his neighbor," for we are members of one another. "Be angry, and do not sin": do not let the sun go down on your wrath, nor give place to the devil. Let him who stole steal no longer, but rather let him labor, working with his hands what is good, that he may have something to give him who has need. Let no corrupt word proceed out of your mouth, but what is good for necessary edification, that it may impart grace to the hearers. And do not grieve the Holy Spirit of God, by whom you were sealed for the day of redemption. Let all bitterness, wrath, anger, clamor, and evil speaking be put away from you, with all malice. And be kind to one another, tenderhearted, forgiving one another, even as God in Christ forgave you.

GROUP QUESTIONS:

1. What does it mean to you personally to be forgiven by God?

2. Who do you need to forgive?

3. What keeps you from forgiving them?

4. How does being forgiven make it possible for us to forgive others?

5. In what ways have you observed your words tear down instead of build up?

6. In what areas of your life have you seen the cycle of bitterness outlined in Ephesians 4:32?

7. How can you break that cycle?

PRAYER:

- Thank God for the forgiveness of sin against him.

- Pray that the Holy Spirit will reveal to us who we need to forgive and who we need to ask to forgive us.

- Pray that we will walk in forgiveness through the power of Jesus in our lives.

EXPERIENCE:

Ephesians 4:25-32 exhorts us to forgive in light of the forgiveness we have received in Jesus. For many of us the inability to forgive or receive forgiveness is what inhibits us from truly living in light of our identity in Jesus.

For our experience this week, prayerfully consider who you need to forgive and who you might need to ask for forgiveness. Take time to write a letter to each person you think of who falls into these categories.

As we learned from the chapter, we can forgive even if the offender does not request it, and we can be forgiven by God even if someone against whom we have sinned withholds forgiveness. Therefore, if the person is accessible, set up a time to meet with him or her to share your letter, or mail it. If the individual is unavailable or it is not safe to contact him or her, then pray through the letter with God.

Enjoy the freedom of giving and receiving forgiveness.

WEEK 13
I AM ADOPTED

INTRODUCTION:

In the first half of Ephesians 5, Paul reminded us that we are children of God, adopted by a benevolent Father who lavishes us with kindness. This adoption gives us a new identity in the Father, through which we now live. No longer enslaved to sin, we're freed to imitate the graciousness, generosity, and holiness of our Dad, all of which are made possible by the life, death, and resurrection of Jesus, who ushered us into the family of God. In light of that, we're invited to share our lives with our brothers and sisters.

Many people today see the church as some kind of club to join. But this isn't a biblical picture at all. Instead, we are adopted into a family. Take time this week to discuss what it means to literally be adopted into a family. Consider how well we are doing as a community in treating one another as brothers and sisters rather then acquaintances or even friends.

Additionally, consider what it means to be a child of the King of kings. How does that affect the way we live our lives and the decisions we make?

VIDEO RESPONSE:

What images do you think of when you hear the term *adoption*?

REVIEW:

Discuss what you experienced last week through the letters of forgiveness that you wrote. How did that experience affect your understanding of the forgiveness God gave to you? How does experiencing such forgiveness free you to live out of your identity in Jesus?

SMALL GROUP STUDY

SCRIPTURE READING:
Ephesians 5:1–21

Therefore be imitators of God as dear children. And walk in love, as Christ also has loved us and given Himself for us, an offering and a sacrifice to God for a sweet-smelling aroma. But fornication and all uncleanness or covetousness, let it not even be named among you, as is fitting for saints; neither filthiness, nor foolish talking, nor coarse jesting, which are not fitting, but rather giving of thanks. For this you know, that no fornicator, unclean person, nor covetous man, who is an idolater, has any inheritance in the kingdom of Christ and God. Let no one deceive you with empty words, for because of these things the wrath of God comes upon the sons of disobedience. Therefore do not be partakers with them. For you were once darkness, but now you are light in the Lord. Walk as children of light (for the fruit of the Spirit is in all goodness, righteousness, and truth), finding out what is acceptable to the Lord. And have no fellowship with the unfruitful works of darkness, but rather expose them. For it is shameful even to speak of those things which are done by them in secret. But all things that are exposed are made manifest by the light, for whatever makes manifest is light. Therefore He says:

> *"Awake, you who sleep,*
> *Arise from the dead,*
> *And Christ will give you light."*

See then that you walk circumspectly, not as fools but as wise, redeeming the time, because the days are evil. Therefore do not be unwise, but understand what the will of the Lord is. And do not be drunk with wine, in which is dissipation; but be filled with the Spirit, speaking to one another in psalms and hymns and spiritual songs, singing and making melody in your heart to the Lord, giving thanks always for all things to God the Father in the name of our Lord Jesus Christ, submitting to one another in the fear of God.

GROUP QUESTIONS:

1. How does your experience with your earthly father affect your understanding as God as father?

2. How does understanding your identity as an adopted child of God change the way you live day to day?

3. Because of what Christ has done for us, we are empowered to live the Christian life. How does what Christ has done make living a life of holiness possible without it becoming a burden?

4. We have an inheritance in Jesus. How does knowing that affect your anxiety level about temporal things?

5. The people of God are a family of brothers and sisters united in Christ. Does your community feel like a family? Why or why not?

6. We are the children of God. How does that affect how your life is lived? What changes?

PRAYER:

- Thank God for adopting us out of a life bent on destruction and making us his children and heirs.

- Pray that the Holy Spirit will give us a passion for Jesus that will make living a life of holiness an outpouring of worship rather than mere rule keeping and religious effort.

- Pray for your orphaned neighbors, that God will graciously adopt them through the work of Jesus.

EXPERIENCE:

Ephesians 5 reminds us that we are children of God and concludes by calling us to "*be filled with the Spirit, speaking to one another in psalms and hymns and spiritual songs, singing and making melody in your heart to the Lord, giving thanks always for all things to God the Father in the name of our Lord Jesus Christ, submitting to one another in the fear of God*" (vv. 18–21). In light of this, plan an afternoon time when you can come together as a group and have an old-fashioned worship night. Get someone who can actually play guitar or a piano, and (don't forget song sheets) sing songs to Jesus. Build a bonfire, head to the beach, play on the apartment roof . . . whatever fits your community. Sometimes we can get in a rhythm of thinking we are too cool for such things but Paul reminded us that this is what the family of God does together. So round up a guitar, and lift up your voices to our King, Jesus.

WEEK 14
I AM LOVED

INTRODUCTION:

If you've ever been to a Christian wedding, you know that Ephesians 5:22–23 is a fairly well-known passage. These verses are definitely helpful in understanding how husbands and wives should love one another. But we'll miss the point if we ignore what this scripture reveals to us about the love that Jesus has for his church.

Jesus loves the church as a husband loves his bride. He sacrifices for her, cleanses her, and presents her as blameless.

Paul's marriage metaphor may seem like a foreign concept in a culture with a distorted view of marriage. Marriage is often seen as an old-fashioned institution that ascribes conditions, expectations, and sometimes abuses to the idea of love. But Jesus cuts through these distortions. Instead, he demonstrates love through perfect action, unconditional and pure.

When we're loved in this kind of efficacious way, we're free to love others in the same way, selflessly and unconditionally. We can reflect Jesus to our spouses, our children, and friends. Because Jesus demonstrated this love even as we rebelled against him, we can also love our enemies.

This week, discuss what it means to be loved by God and how that affects your identity.

READING RESPONSE:

We talk about love a lot in our culture. What do you think of when someone mentions love?

REVIEW:

Discuss what you thought about praising Jesus in song as a family last week. How did that reinforce your identity in Christ?

SCRIPTURE READING:

Ephesians 5:22–33

Wives, submit to your own husbands, as to the Lord. For the husband is head of the wife, as also Christ is head of the church; and He is the Savior of the body. Therefore, just as the church is subject to Christ, so let the wives be to their own husbands in everything. Husbands, love your wives, just as Christ also loved the church and gave Himself for her, that He might sanctify and cleanse her with the washing of water by the word, that He might present her to Himself a glorious church, not having spot or wrinkle or any such thing, but that she should be holy and without blemish. So husbands ought to love their own wives as their own bodies; he who loves his wife loves himself. For no one ever hated his own flesh, but nourishes and cherishes it, just as the Lord does the church. For we are members of His body, of His flesh and of His bones. "For this reason a man shall leave his father and mother and be joined to his wife, and the two shall become one flesh." This is a great mystery, but I speak concerning Christ and the church. Nevertheless let each one of you in particular so love his own wife as himself, and let the wife see that she respects her husband.

GROUP QUESTIONS:

1. People long to be loved. How does our culture reflect this?

2. Where have you seen a longing to be loved manifest in your own life?

3. Do you feel the reality of being loved by God in your life?

4. Are you comforted by the fact that Jesus loves like a groom? How?

5. How does being loved empower you to love others?

6. Where is God calling you to love as he has loved you?

PRAYER:

- Thank God for his unconditional love.

- Pray for opportunities to love one another as a reflection of God's love for us.

- Pray for those who have yet to feel the love of God in and around our community, that God will make that experience real for them.

EXPERIENCE:

This week's scripture reading reminds us that we are loved by God. In chapter 14 of *Who Do You Think You Are?* it is asserted that the world longs for love. This week, keep your eyes open for proof of this claim. Where do you see evidence that the world longs to be loved? How are identities wrapped up in the longing to be loved? Make a list and take pictures of evidence that you come across.

WEEK 15
I AM REWARDED

INTRODUCTION:

Authority is a dirty word in the world today. That's not because authority is inherently evil, but because of our aversion to abuse of power and our rebellious hearts. But loving, biblical authority is a gift from God.

In the first case we rebel against authority because leaders don't always wield authority in a Jesus-honoring way. But it would be a mistake to conclude that all authority is corrupt and to be avoided.

In the second case, we're contending with a sin nature. Apart from Christ we are bent toward rebellion against authority, especially God's.

Our goal this week is to redeem our understanding of authority as it is exercised under the headship of Jesus. This is our goal whether we are in authority or under it, for our relationship to those in authority is a reflection of our submission to God our Father.

Also, according to Ephesians 6:1–9, God uses systems of authority to accomplish his work in the world and to bless his children for their faithfulness regardless of station in life.

VIDEO RESPONSE:

Describe a time when you have been rewarded. What did you do to get rewarded? How did it make you feel to be recognized?

REVIEW:

Discuss what evidence you found last week of a world longing to be loved. How can we use this as a bridge for the gospel into the lives of our friends, neighbors, and coworkers?

SCRIPTURE READING:

Ephesians 6:1–9

Children, obey your parents in the Lord, for this is right. "Honor your father and mother," which is the first commandment with promise: "that it may be well with you and you may live long on the earth." And you, fathers, do not provoke your children to wrath, but bring them up in the training and admonition of the Lord. Bondservants, be obedient to those who are your masters according to the flesh, with fear and trembling, in sincerity of heart, as to Christ; not with eye service, as men-pleasers, but as bondservants of Christ, doing the will of God from the heart, with good-will doing service, as to the Lord, and not to men, knowing that whatever good anyone does, he will receive the same from the Lord, whether he is a slave or free. And you, masters, do the same things to them, giving up threatening, knowing that your own Master also is in heaven, and there is no partiality with Him.

GROUP QUESTIONS:

1. Do you relate more to those in authority or under authority?

2. How does that affect your response to submitting to the authority of Jesus?

3. When you're under authority, how do you honor Christ?

4. When you're in authority, how do you honor Christ?

5. How can we look forward to rewards without them becoming our purpose?

6. Does fear of man affect your ability to be faithful to Jesus? How?

7. How does being rooted in Christ help in overcoming fear?

PRAYER:

- Pray that your community will reflect Jesus to those over whom they have authority.

- Pray that your community will reflect Jesus to those under whose authority they live and work.

- In light of your identity in Christ, pray for boldness in navigating through a culture with a distorted view of authority.

EXPERIENCE:

Set aside some time to meditate through the entire book of Ephesians. Pray through each section and ask God to show you what it means to be his child. Do this each night or morning so that you have read through Ephesians at least four times this week. Keep a notepad handy, and write down any questions about identity in Christ. Share your thoughts and questions with the group the following week.

WEEK 16
I AM VICTORIOUS

INTRODUCTION:

The last section of Ephesians is a reminder of our new identity in Christ and the resulting reconciliation between the Father and one another. At the same time, we're also in opposition with the enemy of God. It's a great comfort to know that "he who is in [us] is greater than he who is in the world" (1 John 4:4 ESV), but we have an enemy nonetheless.

We need to be prepared for war.

John Piper has said that we're falsely convinced that we live in a time of peace rather then acknowledging that we're in a time of spiritual war. Once we wake up to reality, Ephesians reminds us of the weapons of war at our disposal—truth, righteousness, the gospel, faith, salvation, Scripture, and prayer—and that the Christian is empowered to stand firm and hold the line for Jesus.

But it's not as if we're drafted into a conflict without end. No, we're sons and daughters of the King, proclaiming peace and grace to the world as we fight for fellow image bearers deceived by the enemy. Find strength in knowing that Christ and your brothers and sisters in the faith love you. Ultimately, believers are victorious against the enemy because Jesus is victorious over him.

Being rooted in Christ, walk boldly as children of God as he makes his appeal of reconciliation through you. And as Paul wrote in his final prayer for you, *"Peace to the brethren, and love with faith, from God the Father and the Lord Jesus Christ. Grace be with all those who love our Lord Jesus Christ in sincerity. Amen"* (Eph. 6:23–24).

READING RESPONSE:

Describe a time when Christ has been your comfort in the middle of a trial or conflict.

REVIEW:

Watch the final video and discuss what you learned as you meditated through Ephesians last week. Bring your notepad and discuss with the group your questions that have arisen regarding your identity in Jesus.

SCRIPTURE READING:

Ephesians 6:10–24

Finally, my brethren, be strong in the Lord and in the power of His might. Put on the whole armor of God, that you may be able to stand against the wiles of the devil. For we do not wrestle against flesh and blood, but against principalities, against powers, against the rulers of the darkness of this age, against spiritual hosts of wickedness in the heavenly places. Therefore take up the whole armor of God, that you may be able to withstand in the evil day, and having done all, to stand. Stand therefore, having girded your waist with truth, having put on the breastplate of righteousness, and having shod your feet with the preparation of the gospel of peace; above all, taking the shield of faith with which you will be able to quench all the fiery darts of the wicked one. And take the helmet of salvation, and the sword of the Spirit, which is the word of God; praying always with all prayer and supplication in the Spirit, being watchful to this end with all perseverance and supplication for all the saints—and for me, that utterance may be given to me, that I may open my mouth boldly to make known the mystery of the gospel, for which I am an ambassador in chains; that in it I may speak boldly, as I ought to speak.

But that you also may know my affairs and how I am doing, Tychicus, a beloved brother and faithful minister in the Lord, will make all things known to you; whom I have sent to you for this very purpose, that you may know our affairs, and that he may comfort your hearts. Peace to the brethren, and love with faith, from God the Father and the Lord Jesus Christ. Grace be with all those who love our Lord Jesus Christ in sincerity. Amen.

GROUP QUESTIONS:

1. Why is it important to be aware of our enemy and to understand his tactics?

2. Some Christian traditions downplay or even dismiss the reality of the demonic. What is your background, and how does it affect your reading of Ephesians 6:10–24?

3. Is the armor of God offensive or defensive in nature?

4. What does that tell us about how we are to use them?

5. In light of the context of Ephesians, is the armor of God something we put on as individuals or as a community?

6. How does your answer affect your confidence in facing the enemy?

7. Are you encouraged and emboldened by the words of Paul in Ephesians 6:10–24? How?

PRAYER:

- Thank God for freely giving believers new identities in Jesus.

- Thank God for equipping you with perseverance until he returns in glory.

- Thank God for the equipping of his armor, and ask for the Holy Spirit's prompting to remember that you're not without help.

EXPERIENCE:

This week take the time to review what you have learned about finding your identity in Jesus. Journal what that might look like in the next season as it manifests itself in:

- worship to Jesus
- community with the church
- missions to the lost

NOTES

1. 1 Corinthians 13:1–3.
2. Philippians 3:9–11.

WOMEN'S MINISTRY STUDY

WEEK 1

INTRODUCTION

The Inductive Study

Welcome to the Women's Ministry Study. To do an inductive study means to use the Bible as the primary tool to learn about God and receive instruction in how we are to live. Our goals in doing this study are to observe the text, to listen to the Holy Spirit as he leads us to make interpretations, and to apply God's Word to our lives.

The steps are simple. First, begin your time by reading through the assigned scripture and pray in light of what the passage is communicating. Pray that God will open your hearts and minds to learn more about him. Next, examine the text of scripture, in light of the context in which it was written, with an eye on the whole of Scripture. Then zero in on the words on the page. Good questions to ask as you study will be *who, what, where, when, why,* and *how.* Here are some examples of how you might use these kinds of questions:

- Who was the writer's original audience?

- What issue was being addressed? What is being said?

- Where and when did this take place?

- Why was this message being given?

- How was the message being communicated?

The interpretation will come from the text that is before us, as guided by the Holy Spirit, who opens our eyes and reveals what we need to see. Again, please pray that God will be guiding your mind as you examine the text. Keep in mind that as we study Ephesians (as with any book or epistle), it's important to follow the text and let it define the context and audience *before* we jump into our own life application. That's where the above-mentioned questions are so helpful. Who were the Ephesians? What struggles and hardships were they facing? How did Paul address the Ephesian church? What facet of the good news did Paul highlight, and why?

Finally, pay attention to where God is stirring and convicting your heart. This is where we apply the Word to our lives and we're changed into more Christlikeness and our relationship with God is deepened.

INTRODUCTION TO EPHESIANS

Paul's First Missionary Journey (Acts 13:4–14:26)

C. A.D. 46–47

Barnabas and Paul first visited Barnabas's home region of Cyprus before sailing to the southern region of Asia Minor. When they reached Perga in Pamphylia, John Mark left the group and returned to Jerusalem. Making their way to Antioch (in Pisidia), Iconium, Lystra, and Derbe, Paul and Barnabas were driven out of each city by jealous Jewish religious leaders. Later they returned by the same route, strengthening the new churches as they went. From Attalia they set sail for their home in Antioch of Syria.

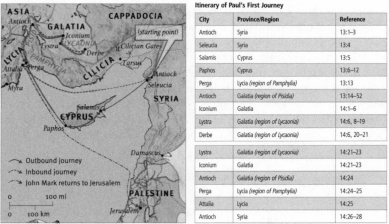

Itinerary of Paul's First Journey

City	Province/Region	Reference
Antioch	Syria	13:1–3
Seleucia	Syria	13:4
Salamis	Cyprus	13:5
Paphos	Cyprus	13:6–12
Perga	Lycia (region of Pamphylia)	13:13
Antioch	Galatia (region of Pisidia)	13:14–52
Iconium	Galatia	14:1–6
Lystra	Galatia (region of Lycaonia)	14:6, 8–19
Derbe	Galatia (region of Lycaonia)	14:6, 20–21
Lystra	Galatia (region of Lycaonia)	14:21–23
Iconium	Galatia	14:21–23
Antioch	Galatia (region of Pisidia)	14:24
Perga	Lycia (region of Pamphylia)	14:24–25
Attalia	Lycia	14:25
Antioch	Syria	14:26–28

Outbound journey
Inbound journey
John Mark returns to Jerusalem

0   100 mi
0   100 km

Imagine walking from Seattle southeast to Albuquerque, New Mexico; west to Orange County, California; and back up to Portland, Oregon. If you walked that distance—approximately 3,200 miles—averaging the ancient Romans' traditional 20 miles per day, your trip would take you 160 days. Yet, this is only a third of the distance that the apostle Paul traveled over the course of his three missionary journeys! Those 3,200 miles are roughly the same distance he traversed on his third missionary journey alone, when he ministered specifically to the Ephesian church. The sacrifice of time, the opposition he withstood at many points, including being beaten, imprisoned,

Paul's Second Missionary Journey (Acts 15:36–18:22)
C. A.D. 49–51

Paul and Silas revisited the places in Asia Minor where Paul had preached on his first journey (cf. map, p. 2110), while Barnabas took John Mark and sailed to Cyprus. Paul and Silas visited Derbe, Lystra, and Antioch in Pisidia. From there Paul and Silas traveled to Troas, where Paul received a vision of a man from Macedonia calling to them. Crossing into Europe, they passed through several towns along the Egnatian Way and traveled to the cities of Athens and Corinth in southern Greece. Then, sailing to Ephesus and Caesarea, they visited the church in Jerusalem before returning to Antioch of Syria.

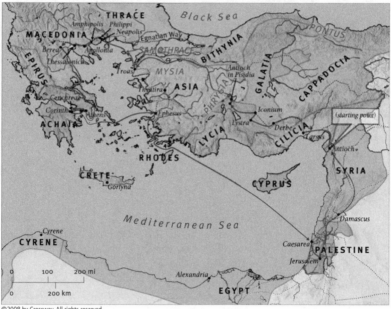

shipwrecked, often short of food . . . all of these are very difficult for us to imagine from a Western culture vantage point. Yet, just contemplating the magnitude of the distance Paul walked on his three missionary journeys— roughly 11,000 miles—can put sacrifice, calling, and love into perspective. Why did Paul do it? He said in Ephesians 1:1 that it was by the will of God, and further in Ephesians 2:10 that these were works that God had laid out for him to do.

Paul's Third Missionary Journey (Acts 18:22–21:17)
c. A.D. 52–57
Paul's third missionary journey traversed much the same ground as his second (cf. map, p. 2118). Passing through Galatia and Phrygia, he proceeded directly to the great port city of Ephesus. After three years of preaching and teaching there, Paul traveled again through Macedonia and Achaia, strengthening the believers, and then finished with a visit to Jerusalem.

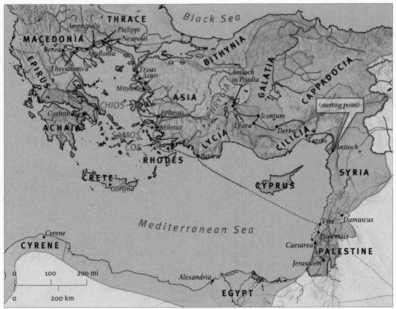

BACKGROUND AND OBSERVATION

Throughout our study of Ephesians we will occasionally turn to other books in the Bible to gain greater clarity on what occurred during Paul's writing and ministry to Ephesus.

Here we are going to take a quick look at Acts for insight into the disciples Paul encountered in Ephesus, the temple of Artemis, and the opposition Paul faced as he preached the gospel of Jesus.

202

We first see Paul in Ephesus at the end of his second missionary journey, when he stopped briefly in Ephesus on his way from Corinth to Judea and Antioch (Acts 18:19–21). He left Aquila and Priscilla in Ephesus, where they met with Apollos, a Jew who was proclaiming boldly that Jesus was the Christ (Acts 18:24–28).

Paul's third missionary voyage, beginning in Antioch, was largely spent with the Ephesian church and the many people who flocked there, as it was a major governmental center of the province of Asia, a wealthy commercial center, and a place of pilgrimage for the worship of Artemis and various Roman emperors.

1. Read Acts 19:1–7.

What was the first interaction Paul had with some disciples in Ephesus? What was missing from their faith?

2. Paul explained to the disciples that there were two different kinds of baptism, one of repentance of sin and one of the receiving of the Holy Spirit. We see in this text that John had baptized the twelve disciples with the baptism of repentance. The disciples knew that John pointed beyond himself to Jesus and that his purpose was to get the people ready for the coming of the Messiah by acknowledging their sin. The disciples probably knew of Jesus' life and ministry and his death and resurrection, but apparently they knew nothing of Pentecost (the outpouring of the Holy Spirit on the disciples of Jesus after his ascension; see Acts 1–2 for more). This lack of knowledge could have developed because they (or their teachers) left Jerusalem shortly after the Passover feast, which explains why they learned of Jesus' death and resurrection, but not of the coming of the Spirit. Paul explained that through baptism in the name of Jesus, the disciples (and believers) would receive the Holy Spirit and his gifts. In some ways, they were like people who are born in a religious home, are baptized outwardly as infants, grow up knowing they are sinners, but have not yet been born again inwardly with a new nature by the power of the Holy Spirit.

How did the disciples in Ephesus respond to the apostle Paul's correction?

Why would you want to not only have an outward sign of Christian life (baptism) but also the inward reality (Holy Spirit)?

3. Read Acts 19:8–20.

How long did Paul initially spend teaching in the synagogue? After withdrawing from the synagogue, how long did Paul reason with people in the hall of Tyrannus?

Who heard the word of the Lord? How many people heard the word of the Lord?

4. Read Acts 19:21.

Who guided Paul's resolution to pass through Macedonia, Achaia (Greece), and Jerusalem?

INTERPRETATION

While Paul did not originally establish the Ephesian church—Apollos was first to have preached the gospel there—Paul dedicated two to three years of his ministry there, as well as time spent in prayer and writing his letter to the Ephesians while imprisoned in Rome.

The presence and work of the Holy Spirit permeated Paul's time there, guiding his travels, his words, and his miracles. We can see that the presence and direction of God in working miracles by Paul's hands was powerfully different from the attempt to work without the Holy Spirit by the seven sons of the high priest Sceva (Acts 19:12, 16).

1. What was the difference between Paul's miracles and the attempted exorcism of the sons of Sceva? What happened to the sons of Sceva? List five ways this affected the community.

APPLICATION

1. When you look at your own life, do you notice the presence or absence of the person and power of the Holy Spirit? Do you tend to overlook the significance and power of the Holy Spirit, or do you find yourself relying on him daily? Do you see the Spirit at work in your life and in the lives

around you? If not, how do you pray the Spirit will work in your life and in the lives around you?

2. When Paul encountered opposition, he changed his location slightly from the synagogue to the hall of Tyrannus, but he did not stop preaching the gospel, as he had been called to do. Do you share the gospel? How do you respond to opposition when you share the gospel?

3. Paul took the time to teach and instruct the disciples. The church grew in depth and number, through the spread of shared life and wisdom. Who has God placed around you? Are you being deliberate about making disciples? With whom is God leading you to share life and the gospel?

4. Paul completely trusted God to direct his path throughout his journeys. Do you see evidence of this same trust in your own life? Do you listen to the Holy Spirit as he directs your steps?

WEEK 2

INTRODUCTION

What do you love? What do you sacrifice for? As the apostle Paul traveled, served, and preached, people sometimes responded in thankfulness and joy at his message, but other times they rioted against him, physically beat him, threatened his life, and eventually killed him. Regardless of people's response, Paul was motivated to continue the mission of the gospel in loving people and sharing the good news of Jesus Christ coming to die for our sins and give us new life in him. Why did Paul do this? What did he love? Paul loved Jesus and trusted that even though circumstances were hard, he would "finish [his] course and the ministry that [he] received from the Lord Jesus" (Acts 20:24 ESV). Paul loved the church and the people that God sent him to serve, to the point that he, following Jesus' example, sacrificed his comfortable life as a wealthy and prominent Pharisee in order to serve them through the power and direction of the Holy Spirit.

What do you love? What do you sacrifice for? Do you lay down your life to serve Jesus and his people, the church? What we love drives what we do.

PRAY that God will impress upon your heart the identity, unity, and love for the church that Paul showed us in Ephesians.

BACKGROUND AND OBSERVATION

Ephesus boasted the largest temple of the Greek world, which was dedicated to the goddess Artemis. It was so renowned that it became one of the seven wonders of the ancient world.

1. Read Acts 19:23–41.

Paul encountered intense opposition and rioting from the silversmiths in Ephesus. They were profiting greatly from the sale of their temple relics and were worried and angered over the effect that Paul's ministry was having on their business.

How did Paul's preaching the gospel of Jesus, and the Holy Spirit opening people's hearts to the Word of God, affect the people of Ephesus? Why did

Demetrius object to Paul's teaching? What did he and the Ephesian rioters love?

Who protected Paul?

2. Read Acts 20.

Paul departed from Ephesus for Macedonia and Greece and stopped on several islands, to preach and serve the people of those areas. His goal was to return to Jerusalem for the day of Pentecost (v. 16), yet he took the time to stop in Miletus to meet with the Ephesian elders one more time and to encourage them, knowing that this would be the last time he'd see them (v. 25).

3. Reread Acts 20:17–38.

How did Paul describe his ministry in Ephesus? How did the Holy Spirit guide Paul's steps?

What emotions do you see from Paul toward the elders, and the elders toward Paul?

Paul knew that after he departed, "fierce wolves" would come among the people of Ephesus, seeking to tear down the church by speaking twisted things and pulling the disciples away to follow them instead of Jesus (v. 29 ESV). How did Paul encourage the elders to combat these wolves (20:31–32)?

What words of Jesus did Paul quote?

What effect did Paul's love for the people have on his words and actions in this exchange? How did they show love for one another?

INTERPRETATION

Paul walked and traveled by boat, pouring out his life for the people to whom God directed him to minister. Clearly, the Ephesians were dear to his heart, as they all wept at his departure. This sets the tone for Paul's letter to the Ephesians—that Paul was well loved by the people and that he had pastored them well. The things we love motivate how we act and how we treat the people around us.

Paul's love for the people contrasts strongly with the Ephesian rioters' love for their income and the traditions of serving their idols. In many ways we are just like the Ephesian rioters: when faced with the truth of the gospel, we cling to our income, our comforts, and our traditions (among other things), instead of repenting.

1. Is God telling you to give any of these things up right now? How are you being invited to love and trust in him more fully?

APPLICATION

1. When you first believed in Jesus, was there something radical from which you walked away?

2. Like the Ephesians' riot against Paul's teaching, what "riot" against God are you waging in your heart right now? What do you think you have been deprived of by God? Do you feel entitled to something? Are you responding to a perceived injustice?

3. What happens when you are rioting? What does it show about what you love?

4. As we read how Paul laid down his life for the Ephesian believers, even to the point of death, we are reminded of Paul's model in Jesus, who laid down his life for us. Do you know that Jesus died on the cross for your sins so that you might be given a new life in Christ? If you would like to learn more about this, please, please, talk to your table leader.

5. If you have placed your trust in Jesus, how are you being asked to lay down your life in love to sacrifice for those around you?

6. Put yourself in the shoes of an Ephesian church member. If you had this relationship with a loving pastor like Paul, how would you receive Paul's letter? Are you praying that God will speak to you directly through Paul's letter to the Ephesians?

WEEK 3

READ EPHESIANS 1:1–2.

When you write a letter to someone, or when you send an e-mail, how do you sign your name? How do you define yourself on your Facebook profile?

In scripture, your name is not just a title or what people call you; it is part of your identity. Paul opened the book of Ephesians by naming himself "Paul an apostle of Christ Jesus by the will of God" (1:1 ESV). He could have said "Paul of Tarsus," or "The man formerly known as Saul," but those names are not complete. Paul's identity was that of an apostle of Jesus—one who is sent to do Jesus' work by the will of God, who sent him. In doing so, Paul laid down his life to continually serve the people of God.

The book of Ephesians is a call for the people of the church to identify with Christ in unity as his bride. We do so as we claim an identity in Jesus, rather than in any other way we could name ourselves.

OBSERVATION

1. What is Paul's tone in these two verses?

2. The opening of Paul's letter to the Ephesians follows the typical Jewish letter of Paul's day, declaring the sender and the addressee. How did Paul describe himself? Who had given Paul the job of apostle and the authority to write this letter?

3. What does the word *saint* mean? Where were the saints?

4. What does the word *faithful* mean? In what ways were the saints faithful?

5. In verse 2, what does *grace* mean? What does *peace* mean? Where do grace and peace come from?

INTERPRETATION

1. In the midst of his time in Ephesus, Paul served "the Lord with all humility and with tears and with trials" (Acts 20:19 ESV), yet he said that to him "this grace was given, to preach to the Gentiles the unsearchable

riches of Christ" (Eph. 3:8 ESV). And yet Paul underwent severe trials throughout his ministry. In 2 Corinthians 11:25–28 Paul summarized his sufferings for the sake of the gospel. How does suffering fit together with God's grace for Paul?

2. A major emphasis in Ephesians is grace—God's unmerited favor toward sinners. This truth is the bedrock of everything else that follows in the epistle. Paul prayed fervently that the Ephesians would have the eyes of their hearts enlightened to comprehend the depth of God's love and the inheritance that they possessed in the person and work of Jesus.

Out of this depth of understanding, there was unity in the body of Christ between Jews and Greeks. As that was established, Paul gave the Ephesians instruction for how to live in light of that unity in the church, in the family, in marriage, and in general relationships.

In our culture, grace is often translated as beauty, poise, or the attractiveness of the one that is "graced." But biblically defined, grace doesn't have anything to do with a personal virtue that is earned. Rather, grace is bestowed. Steve Brown says, "Scripture says that grace isn't a personal virtue at all; but, rather, undeserved favor lavished on an inferior by a superior."[1]

Reflecting on what you've read the last two weeks in Acts, and on the rest of Ephesians—particularly 1:7; 2:5–8, 14; and 3:1–8—what grace and peace were evident in Paul's life?

APPLICATION

1. Paul spent the first half of Ephesians examining the believer's standing in Christ. Not only are we blessed with every spiritual blessing, but the first half of Ephesians rings with how God has loved us and called us to himself. How have you responded to God's call?

2. As saints of God, we are chosen, holy, blameless before him, predestined, adopted, beloved, redeemed, forgiven, and lavished upon. Who we are in Christ is cause for thankfulness and rejoicing!

The text says that saints were both "in Ephesus" and "in Christ Jesus." Based on the context of the rest of Ephesians, which identity is predominant, the Ephesians' identity as citizens of Ephesus, or their identity "in Christ"?

Think about where you live and the things that identify you. Which identity is predominant for you?

3. How have you experienced God's grace and peace? If you haven't, and if God is stirring your heart to know more about him, please talk to your leader. If you have accepted Jesus as Lord of your life, REJOICE, for you are chosen, holy, blameless before him, predestined, adopted, beloved, redeemed, forgiven, and lavished upon! Take the time to think about what each of these words means (see Ephesians 1:3–12).

WEEK 4

READ EPHESIANS 1:3–14.

On the way home from church one Sunday, I asked my three-year-old daughter how her time in kids church was. The entire twenty-minute ride home, she went on in an epic run-on sentence detailing every activity and how much she liked it. Imagine the apostle Paul in the same way, so completely overjoyed with the blessings of God that one simple sentence wouldn't suffice to adequately convey his excitement.

This passage packs a punch. These eleven verses begin as a blessing, touch on the basic tenets of Christian theology, and introduce themes and key phrases that will repeat throughout the rest of Ephesians. In the original Greek, this passage is one long run-on sentence of 202 words. In English translations, it is dense in wording and yet rich in meaning.

OBSERVATION

Let's begin with some general questions.

1. What is the big idea of this passage?

2. If you were to write a header for this section of scripture, how would you title it in your own words?

3. What are the major idea, truths, or doctrines mentioned?

4. Why did Paul write this passage?

INTERPRETATION

1. Write down every blessing Paul mentioned that believers receive from God through Jesus. Look for instances where the text mentions God or his actions for us, (as in verse 4: "He chose us") as well as when *we* or *you* is followed by the word *have* (as in verse 7: "we have redemption").

2. Ephesians 1:3–14 introduces us to a common phrase in the writings of Paul: "in Christ." In fact, the phrase "in Christ," and the variants "in Him" and "in the Beloved," saturate this chapter.

Note each mention of "in Christ" (or "in Him" or "in the Beloved"); what do you learn about Paul's use of this phrase?

The phrase "in Christ" occurs almost exclusively in the writings of Paul, over 200 times. Paul loved this phrase and used it often. In our passage of study, "in Christ" is mostly used to describe how God acts. Christ is the instrument through which he blesses, chooses, adopts, redeems, and forgives us.

The disciple John was the only other New Testament author to use the phrasing "in Christ." In John 15, John reported what Jesus said in relation to being "in" him in the imagery of branches connected to the vine. So there are two senses in which we are "in Christ." On the one hand, Jesus purchased our redemption on the cross, and that was accomplished outside of our experience. We receive God's blessings "in" Christ by being the recipients of predestination, adoption, redemption, forgiveness, etc. We are also "in" Christ in the sense of branches connected to a vine, and unified with him, by the Spirit (John 17:23).

Paul articulated how God blesses us in Christ. Those blessings come through the Holy Spirit. Paul then concluded the reading with another bookend emphasis on the Holy Spirit being the guarantee, sign, and seal of our inheritance.

3. How is the Holy Spirit described in verses 13–14? What are his purposes? When do we receive him? Why is he important? What does it mean to be sealed with the Holy Spirit, and what are the results of that in the life of a believer?

APPLICATION

1. Find a conversation partner, preferably someone you don't know well, and do the following exercise together.

First, answer these questions: Are you tempted to take on an identity contrary to Ephesians 1:3–14. What is that false identity?

As a way to gain clarity on what this false identity may be, use two columns to show the benefits of being in Christ (being blessed, chosen, holy, blameless, predestined, adopted, redeemed, forgiven, a recipient of a glorious inheritance, lavished with grace, etc.) versus the opposite of being "in Christ."

2. What "anti-gospel" truth do you struggle with? Does the truth of God's Word of being "in Christ" convict, or encourage you?

3. What assurance does being sealed with the Spirit provide you? How does this change you and practically apply to your daily life?

FOR FURTHER STUDY:

1. If I asked you to "count your blessings," what blessings would make your list?

After reading Paul's lists of the blessings God has given us in Christ, does the term *blessing* have new meaning to you? If so, what?

2. Divide Ephesians 1:3–14 into phrases. Then in prayer, meditate on each phrase, praising God for the truth within, and ask the Holy Spirit to make each phrase come alive to you. For example, Ephesians 1:3–4 (ESV) would be broken down into the following phrases:

> Blessed be the God and Father of our Lord Jesus Christ,
> > who has blessed us in Christ with every spiritual blessing in the heavenly places,
> > even as he chose us in him before the foundation of the world,
> > that we should be holy and blameless before him.

3. In a journal, write the heading "In Christ." Catalog all you have learned in this lesson that we possess "in Christ." Add to the list as we continue our study of Ephesians. Consider this your new ID card, and pray through the list periodically that the Holy Spirit will help you recognize and claim the true identity you have in Jesus.

This portion of scripture is full of identity language, and the application should be very practical. Keep a running list of blessings, and see if your definition of blessing changes (according to scripture, trials are a blessing too).

4. While we often think of blessings in the physical sense, Ephesians 1:3–14 bombards us with a list of blessings, like predestination, election, adoption, redemption, forgiveness, and inheritance, just to name a few. These blessings can seem like heady, theological concepts. But it's important to absorb these glorious truths and not passively take them for granted.

Using a Bible dictionary, write in your own words definitions for the following:

Gospel
Doctrine
Holy
Predestination
Election
Adoption
Redemption
Forgiveness
Reconciliation

WEEK 5

READ EPHESIANS 1:15–23.

Firsthand, real-world experience goes a long way, especially when it comes to life before the face of God.

To have a truly deep understanding of something new, many layers of learning have to take place. There are things that we can understand up to a point, but there's no shortcut to firsthand knowledge. You can learn how to change a tire from a manual, but actually changing it can be a challenge. You could also learn about a new food from reading a restaurant review, but nothing compares to an actual experience. We have limited knowledge until we've had to change a tire in the pouring rain, and until you've tasted the delicious food that review raved about.

Head knowledge is helpful, but real-world experiences shape your person.

This was the apostle Paul's longing for the Ephesian church—that they would not merely have a head knowledge, but would taste and see that the Lord is good. Paul saw the church's faithfulness but wanted them to experience God's goodness firsthand. Paul himself had known God and his promises and wanted the same for the Ephesians. Through experiential knowledge, the Ephesians would be changed as they enjoyed their glorious inheritance as children of God.

Paul appreciated the Ephesian saints' faithfulness and prayed that they would gain wisdom and understanding of their glorious inheritance in Christ. The second half of this passage is a gospel proclamation drawing on the importance of Jesus' work on the cross.

OBSERVATION

Paul prayed for the Ephesians to receive Holy Spirit–imparted knowledge of the power available through Jesus' work on the cross.

1. What words and actions did Paul use to describe the Ephesians?

2. Does the Bible speak of this kind of believer elsewhere? (Read 2 Thessalonians 1:3 to discover another place this is mentioned in Scripture.)

3. What requests did Paul pray for these believers?

4. What is promised to the believer (Eph. 1:18), and how is it obtained (v. 20)?

INTERPRETATION

God gives good gifts to his children, by the Spirit, through the work and authority of King Jesus. God gives wisdom and revelation, and enlightens us by the Spirit with the knowledge of the immeasurable riches we have in Jesus.

So much of what we need daily for the Christian life is already completed. We need to pray that God will direct our hearts to see and gain wisdom, in light of what Jesus has done on the cross.

Study through these scriptures and "see" what God shows you.

1. What is the message God desires us to know in this particular passage?

2. How many different names did God use for himself in this passage? How does this change in the passage?

3. What is the "glorious inheritance" that Paul was speaking about (Eph. 1:18 ESV)?

4. What is the "spirit of wisdom" (v. 17)? Where else is the "spirit of wisdom" used in the Bible? (Hint: Isaiah 11:2.)

5. How does God accomplish all this work?

APPLICATION

Through this scripture God calls Christians to reflect on who we are already in Christ. He needed no action from us to complete his work. We are to merely meditate on the vast nature of his work.

a) How does this scripture change the way I think? What feels hard to understand?

b) "He put all things under his feet and gave him as head over all things to the church" (Eph. 1:22 ESV). What is your heart response to knowing this about Jesus? How does your life look different because of this truth?

James 1:22 says, "But be doers of the word, and not hearers only, deceiving yourselves." Paul desired the same thing for the Ephesian church: that they would listen to the Word and do what it says. But before Paul called us to Christian duty, he lavished the Ephesian saints with the depth of riches that they possessed in Christ.

1. Paul gave us a glimpse into his prayer life. He "[did] not cease" and he "[made] mention" of the Ephesians in his prayers. Has someone blessed you by praying without ceasing? Who is someone that you can bless through your vigilant prayers?

2. Paul said that he heard of the Ephesians' faith in Jesus and love for all the saints. Would someone say this about your church or about your life? Why or why not?

3. Many times we read too quickly over the introductions of Paul's letters. Have you become overly familiar with the hope that you have because of the riches of your glorious inheritance and the power that flows from knowing about them? Is there anything in this passage with which you have become too familiar?

FOR FURTHER STUDY

Write out each verse and paraphrase Ephesians 1:15–23 in your own words.

List what you are currently struggling with in life. How does deeply knowing and understanding that you have received the riches of an inheritance in Christ give you a different perspective amid your struggle?

WEEK 6

READ EPHESIANS 2:1–10.

I recently heard someone say that babies are born innocent and perfect, and that the bad that we do is something we learn from our parents and society. But is this really true? Sometimes I wonder if people who make these statements have actually observed children at play. One story of my two young nephews comes to mind.

The younger brother, who was three at the time, was playing in the backyard with his older brother. Playtime was fine until the older brother didn't get his way and he kicked his brother with full force in the face. I can assure you that neither of his parents had ever kicked each other in the face, so where did this little boy learn that behavior?

Scripture says that God did in fact create humankind good and without a sin nature. "Then God said, 'Let us make man in Our image, according to Our likeness' . . . God created man in His own image, in the image of God He created him; male and female He created them" (Gen. 1:26–27). The problem is, in Genesis 3 Adam and Eve disobeyed God, sin entered the world, and Adam and Eve's sin nature was passed on to their children, unhappily ever after. As sons and daughters of Adam and Eve, we enter the world spiritually dead, with no preference or fondness for God. Restored communion with our Creator God requires salvation by grace through faith.

OBSERVATION

In Ephesians 2:1 Paul exuberantly detailed God's plan for believers and the miracle of salvation. He also delivered some bad news: that before faith, every believer is dead in trespasses and sin and under the influence of Satan. The severity of our condition highlights the wonder of God's mercy when he comes to our rescue and gives us a new life! But this is not of our own doing, as verse 10 makes clear. We are saved by God's grace, and created in Christ for good works. If we were created by him and for him, then the power to do good works comes from him as well. God's grace changes our hearts, thoughts, and actions and enables us to accomplish that which we never would have been able to on our own.

Read Ephesians 2:1; Romans 5:12; 6:4; John 3:3.

1. What do these verses say about our condition outside of Christ?

2. What does it mean to be spiritually dead? *no purpose / separate from God*

3. What blessings do we receive by being alive in Christ?

INTERPRETATION

Throughout the Bible God took sinners, redeemed them from death to a newness of life in Christ, and gave them an eternal purpose.

This passage highlights the stark contrast between the unworthiness of sinners and God's grace toward them in salvation. While we were still dead in trespasses and sin, God in his grace made a way for us to be reconciled to himself in Christ Jesus. The starkness of dark and light in this passage highlights God's goodness despite human failure in sin.

1. In Ephesians 2:4, what was God's attitude toward those living in sin? *merciful, loving*

2. What does it mean to "walk" in our sin, as mentioned in verse 2? *live in*

3. Verse 4 begins with two words: "But God." How do those two words affect our salvation? *God's doing, not our doing*

4. Verses 1 and 5 say we are made alive in Christ. Whose authority are believers given over the spiritual influences in this world?

5. Read Ephesians 1:6–7 and Romans 3:24; 5:2. What does Ephesians 1:5–6 say about being saved by grace, and what does that mean?

APPLICATION

Ephesians 2:10 describes Christians as God's workmanship. The Greek word for this means: "to make, to practice, to produce, to create." It is the Greek word *poi/hma* from which we get the word *poem*. "Genesis 2:7 says that God breathed the breath of life into man. We are literally "God breathed," and because we are God's workmanship, our salvation cannot be of ourselves. It is God who creates and saves, and we are the work of his hands, ourselves created to abound in good works. The power to do these good works comes from the Holy Spirit. The same power that caused Jesus to rise from death lives in us, enabling us to do his good work.

1. Ephesians 2:10 says we are God's workmanship. What has God given you to be used for his church?

2. Verses 6–10 describe our new identity in Christ. List specific ways Christ has brought you from death to life. In what particular areas or at what times do you still feel entitled to live in the passions of the flesh (see verse 3)?

3. In what specific areas of your life are you in need of God's grace? Would your friends say you give the same grace to others that God gives to you?

4. Ephesians 2:7 describes the immeasurable riches of God's grace in his kindness toward us. Write out the specific areas where God has shown you kindness this week, and share those with others as you feel led.

FOR FURTHER STUDY

1. Read the story of a Pharisee named Nicodemus in John 3:1–15. What does Jesus mean by "born again"?

2. Read about the death of Lazarus in John 11:1–44 and how Jesus raised Lazarus from the dead. To learn more about being raised with Christ, read Colossians 3:1–17.

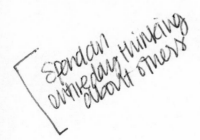

WEEK 7

READ EPHESIANS 2:11–22.

Have you ever felt like an outsider? Maybe growing up you felt different from the other kids, were left out of events, or were always the last one picked to be on the team. Maybe you've been excluded from opportunities or groups because of your gender, race, or socioeconomic status, alienated from others.

In this passage, Paul addressed a group of people in just this position, but far worse—they weren't only separated from other people; they were also separated from God himself. For many years, God's covenant was with the nation of Israel, the Jews. Out of their privileged status, they were called to be a blessing to the nations, but they horded their special rank. This meant that other people, the Gentiles, were seen as second-rate citizens. Let's look together at this division, how Jesus took down the barrier, and how this affects us today.

OBSERVATION

For thousands of years, the Gentiles had experienced separation from God and a hostile relationship with the Jews. The news that Jesus made a way for both of those things to be redeemed was revolutionary to them, almost too good to be true.

Read through the entire section and make some general observations about how Paul communicated this amazing message.

1. Throughout the passage, what words or phrases did Paul use to describe the Gentiles' position before Christ? What did he say about their place after he saves them? *US before reconciliation!*

2. In verse 11, Paul referred to circumcision. Read Genesis 17:1–14. What is circumcision a sign of? Why is this a significant distinction?

3. "Flesh" is mentioned twice in Ephesians 2:11–22 (vv.11,15). To whose flesh was Paul referring, and how are the two different?

4. To what purpose does Paul say that the Jews and Gentiles are made one?

peace, putting death to the enemy

start the church

5. Where do you see the Trinity (Father, Son, and Holy Spirit) referenced in this passage? How do they work together?

6. Is there anything else that stands out to you about how the text was written or to whom it was written?

INTERPRETATION

Before Jesus came, God's people were expected to adhere to "the law of commandments expressed in ordinances" (v.15 ESV). Not only did this demonstrate separation from God (by showing that humans achieving the perfection of God is impossible); it also created a chasm between Jews and Gentiles. By abolishing the law and rendering it powerless to save, he created one people group in place of the two, giving unity to all of his people, Jew and Gentile alike.

1. What message do you think God has for the Gentiles in this passage? The Jews?

2. Why is it significant that Paul was writing this letter? (Hint: read Philippians 3:3–6.)

3. In the "Observation" section, you read Genesis 17:1–14. How is it related to this section? In what way were the Gentiles "strangers to the covenants of promise" (Eph. 2:12 ESV)?

4. Looking again at the English Standard Version, what is the "dividing wall of hostility" mentioned in verse 14? How did breaking it down create "one new man in place of the two" (v. 15)?

5. What is the "peace" that Jesus preached (v. 17)? Why is it needed?

6. Verses 16–18 say that we have been reconciled to the Father and now have access to him in the Spirit through Jesus. According to Romans 5:9–11, how is this possible? What part do we play in this? What would this have meant to the first-century Christians hearing this?

7. What does it mean to be "a holy temple in the Lord" and "a dwelling place of God," with Jesus as the cornerstone?

APPLICATION

It's not only the Gentiles in Ephesus who got to enjoy reconciliation to God and unity with his people—Paul's words are great news for us too! Because of Christ's work and sacrifice on our behalf, we have been grafted into the covenant of God, and are living in unity with the rest of his family.

1. When have you felt farthest from God? What caused you to feel this way? Do your feelings give clues to what you believe about God's character? What do your feelings say about how God sees you?

2. Do you still feel like an outsider in the family of God? What is it about who you are or what you have done that causes these feelings or beliefs? If you are a Christian, you are "in Christ." With that in mind, what barriers that you once hid behind have been removed?

3. Is there something you believe God is asking you to repent of regarding how you have identified yourself outside of him?

4. Ephesians 2:14 tells us that Jesus is our peace. In what other places, things, or people have you sought peace? Why haven't you gone to Jesus as the source of true peace first?

5. In v.18 we are told that we have access through the Holy Spirit to God the Father. What does it mean to you that you have direct access to God? When is it hardest for you to approach God in prayer? Why?

6. Jesus is the cornerstone of the church, of which we are all a part, "grow[ing] into a holy temple in the Lord" (Eph. 2:21). The purpose of a temple, or sanctuary, is worship. How does knowing Jesus is the foundation for your worship, instead of a church, building, leaders, or members, change how you see your worship?

WEEK 8

READ EPHESIANS 3:1–13.

The apostle Paul has a robust backstory. Prior to his conversion on the road to Damascus, Paul (then called Saul) was a Pharisee—and had become a persecutor of the early church of Jesus Christ, breathing threats of murder against the disciples of the Lord. He was an enemy of all who believed that salvation comes through Jesus Christ alone. He had been on a mission to bring these believers, bound in chains, to Jerusalem to be punished. But then he encountered the risen Savior, Jesus Christ, and his grace on that road leading to Damascus, and everything changed. Everything.

In Acts 9:15 we are told that Saul was chosen by God to carry his name before the Gentiles, kings, and children of Israel. Yes, the very same Saul who was on a mission to destroy the early church was now on a mission to share the mystery of the gospel of Jesus Christ with all people, but especially the Gentiles. In Ephesians 3:1–13 Paul wrote about the mystery of the gospel as it was originally revealed to him on the road to Damascus. The mystery that we will unpack together is that Christ has come to unify Jew and Gentile in one body through the gospel.

OBSERVATION

1. Who was the intended audience of this portion of Paul's letter?

2. Why was he writing to them?

3. What point was Paul trying to make in this passage?

4. What are the main ideas and doctrines mentioned in this passage?

5. What words and ideas are repeated?

INTERPRETATION

1. Paul began this chapter with "For this reason, . . ." This phrase points us to previous information as a premise for the section to come. What is "this reason"?

2. As you answer the following questions, remember to look back at some of the repeated words and verses you have noted. This is a way to further understand the big picture and help us grasp the writer's intent.
   What was the mystery that Paul revealed in this passage?
   How was this mystery made known to Paul?
   Where is the Holy Spirit mentioned or implied?
   Where do you see God's grace, for Paul and for the Gentile?

3. Paul told us in verse 5 that the sons of men of other generations did not know this mystery of Christ. To which men was Paul referring, and what was it that they did not know about the Gentiles, in particular? What has changed from their generations?

4. Ephesians 3:12 lists some of the beautiful gifts that are realized for those in Christ Jesus. What are those gifts?

APPLICATION

1. In Ephesians 3:6 Paul made it clear to the Gentiles that they are "fellow heirs, members of the same body, and partakers of the promise in Christ Jesus" (ESV). Paul was definitely speaking to those who had been saved by grace, by Christ's death in their place. Have you heard this news before? Our sin against our Holy God makes us deserving of death, but Jesus bore that death penalty for us on the cross to reconcile us to God, the Father. Do you believe this to be true? Do you trust that God loves you more than you can imagine, no matter what you've done or what has been done to you? If you haven't yet accepted this gift, please talk with your leader about who God is and what he has done for you.

If you are a Christian, what does it mean to you to know, as one possessing eternal salvation, that you can take part in the promises of Christ, and what are those promises for you?

2. Everything God has done, and will do, is for His eternal purpose. Prior to salvation in Christ, we consider our lives to be "our stories." When we receive the gift of salvation through Jesus Christ, our lives become part of "his story." A big part of his story is that he is bringing people of different walks of life together for them to be a witness of his goodness to the watching world, for his glory.

Do you tend to only spend time with people in church who are just like you? Why?

How might fellowship with those different from you be a witness to the world?

This week, how and where can you meet and engage people in your community who are not yet believers?

What does this call to unity in the church say about the character of God?

3. Paul was in prison when he wrote the letter to the Ephesians. Obviously, that meant he was suffering. In the midst of this suffering, he was separated from those he cared about and unable to preach the gospel in person. Even so, he was committed to encouraging them, and exhorted them to "not lose heart" (Eph. 3:13). Our faith in Christ should not be dependent on our circumstances. Our circumstances do not declare our God good or bad—he is always good. Suffering comes with this earthly life, and we can be closer than ever to Jesus in the midst of it.

How do you respond to others in the midst of your own suffering?

When have you "lost heart" in the midst of suffering, and turned toward introspection rather than turning outward toward the hope you have in Jesus?

How did the Holy Spirit remind you of your identity as one of His own?

When has God given you his power to obey him—even in suffering?

Stepping out in faith amid suffering is hard. Have you talked to God about your suffering, and is it possible that there are blessings even within suffering?

FOR FURTHER STUDY

Read Ephesians 3:12. What did Paul mean by having "boldness and access with confidence through faith in Him"?

Why was this necessary to say?

What does it mean for you to be able to approach God because of Jesus?

Do you feel that you can approach God?

Read Hebrews 4:16 for more on this.

WEEK 9

READ EPHESIANS 3:14–21.

Paul concluded this section in Ephesians with a glorious doxology: Now to him who is able to do far more abundantly than all that we ask or think, according to the power at work within us, 21 to him be glory in the church and in Christ Jesus throughout all generations, forever and ever. Amen. (vv. 20–21).

A doxology is an expression of praise to God, especially a short hymn sung as part of a Christian worship service.

Men and women were created to glorify God and enjoy him forever. We were made to worship and praise him. Instead, we often worship everything but our Creator God. Food, sex, drugs, alcohol, exercise, our appearance, busyness, work, reputation, success, etc., all become objects of worship. And we sing more exuberantly and freely at sports games and music concerts than we do in praise to God.

John Piper says:

> There is in the heart of every child and teenager and adult the need and longing to sing a doxology. The main reason people feel awkward about singing or shouting glory to God is simply that he is not as real to them [as someone they admire or respect here on earth]. So the meaning of doxology is clear to anyone who has ever admired anything. You've all done it. But the experience of having your heart soar in admiration to GOD depends on whether you have ears to hear and eyes to see that above and behind every admirable thing on earth stands the magnificence and beauty God.[2]

Paul admired and adored and worshipped God. He couldn't help but sing praises to him, and he was desperate for others to do the same. Paul understood that God's power and love for the church exceeded anything we can ever imagine. But he prayed in Ephesians 3:18–19 that the church would "have power to comprehend with all the saints what is the breadth and length and height and depth, and to know the love of Christ which surpasses knowledge" (ESV).

Let's look at this section together and see if we can grow in understanding and awe of God and his power and love for us, his church.

OBSERVATION

This passage is Paul's prayer for the fellow believers in Ephesus. It reveals both his heart for the people and God's heart for us. It also models for us how, for whom, and for what we should pray. As you read through the passage, dig deeper by asking the following questions:

1. What is this passage about?

2. What words, ideas, or images are repeated?

3. Who is named or referenced? What are they doing?

4. What are we being told to do?

5. What do we need to find out more about?

INTERPRETATION

1. What was the reason Paul was praying for the Ephesians? What does his posture indicate about his desire for the Ephesians? Why is God concerned with the attitudes of our hearts as we come to him in prayer? Can you think of other places in Scripture where someone's physical attitude is significant?

2. In Ephesians 3:14–16, Paul prayed that the Ephesians would be strengthened in the inner man. We cannot stand against sin and temptation without God's strength. This request was made boldly, not like a dog that would get table scraps from the floor, but as a child would ask for a gift from a billionaire father who loves him, knowing the father's riches greatly exceed the child's imaginings. Paul knew that God is generous and has an unending supply of spiritual riches to draw from.

Who makes up the "family" in verse 15? What do you think is meant by "in heaven and earth?" What is the name that identifies the family? Why would this have been a meaningful statement to the Christians at Ephesus?

3. Paul prayed that Christ would dwell and deeply abide in the believers' hearts. This is what would root and ground them in love. If they could gain an experiential understanding that Christ loved them, they would respond in love toward others and have a foundation to respond from when they are sinned against.

Read John 15:1–11. How does this passage enhance your understanding of the Ephesians passage? What similarities do you notice between the two? Why do you think love is such an important component of abiding or dwelling?

4. In v.18-19, Paul says that God's love is beyond our knowledge, understanding, or experience. It is knowing Christ's love, as far as we are able to, that allows us to be filled with the fullness of God through faith.

When Paul referred to the breadth, length, height, and depth of God's love (ESV), do you think he was implying that there are limits to God's love, that it is measurable? What did he mean when he said that we can know something that surpasses knowledge?

5. Verses 20–21 say that God's gifts are received but not attained on our own. Apart from God we cannot be strengthened inwardly, be rooted or grounded in love, or be filled with the fullness of God. With him, even the things that we don't fully understand are a reality for believers. That is why Paul called us to give God the glory.

What does this praise reveal to us about who God is? And how does this affect our prayers to God?

APPLICATION

1. How much attention do you pay to the attitude of your heart and its preparation before you approach the Lord in prayer? What would you like to do differently?

2. Do you pray most often for the physical circumstances and cares of yourself and others, or that the Holy Spirit might strengthen the spirits of those you pray for? What does your current prayer life indicate about your view of God?

3. What does it mean to you to allow Christ to dwell in you? How or in what area would you like to more deeply dwell with Christ?

4. What provides stability in your life? If it is not God, what is more desirable about having your life rooted in that thing or person? What aspects of your life are you hesitant to relinquish control of to Him? Why?

5. The phrase "love of Christ that surpasses knowledge" in the original language refers to a knowledge gained through experience (Eph. 3:19 ESV). When have you experienced the deep love of Christ? How can you be a vehicle for someone else to experience the deep love of Christ? Be specific.

6. Spend some time in prayer asking God to show you how he desires you to grow in faith in this area.

FOR FURTHER STUDY

1. Do a word study on the word "dwell" in verse 17.

2. Compare this prayer with that of Solomon as he dedicated the temple in 1 Kings 8. What similarities and differences do you notice?

3. Rewrite this lesson's passage as a prayer, personalizing it.

WEEK 10

Read Ephesians 4:1–16.

INTRODUCTION

In any family, each member has a part to play. Maybe one person is responsible for making sure there is a steady income to provide for the physical needs of the family. Another might take on managing that income and buy food and clothes for everyone. And still another may have household chores to make sure the living space is clean and orderly. In a healthy family, where things are going well, each of these members plays a different role. If they are all working for the same goal, in love for one another, then they are all moving in sync in the same direction.

The same is true of the family of God. As Christians, we have been given unity through Christ's sacrifice for us and are now under his authority as one family, but we each have a different assignment. In this section, Paul pleaded with the Ephesians to live out this truth. He acknowledged that God had given different gifts and abilities to each of them, but it was all for one purpose: to grow in their faith as a body, and to love one another and serve together toward that goal.

OBSERVATION

One of the ways we can see what is important to Paul is to observe the structure of his letter. In this section in particular, he used several lists to reiterate what he was saying and to make sure his point was clearly understood.

1. What words do you see that mark transitions in the letter?

2. Make a list of the directives you see Paul giving the Ephesians in this section.

3. What other lists did Paul include?

4. What is the "grace" that is referred to in verse 7? When was it given? (Hint: read ahead to verse 8.)

5. Who was doing the equipping, and who was doing the work of ministry?

INTERPRETATION

Ephesians 4 marks a change in the tone of the letter. In the first half, Paul was primarily reminding the church of Jesus' work for them and their position because of it. The second word in chapter 4, "Therefore," is a word of transition. In the second half, Paul gave directives, but it is important to remember what he had said up to this point when reading the final three chapters. These last words are not a list of rules and commands to frantically try to keep, but simply an admonition to live out of the identity that we've been given as believers in Christ.

1. What is the calling that Paul referred to in verse 1? Why did he urge the Ephesians to "walk in a manner worthy" of it (ESV)?

2. For what purpose did Paul say that God gives gifts?

3. What did Paul mean by "speaking the truth in love" (v. 15)?

4. What does it mean to build up the body of Christ (see verses 12, 16)?

APPLICATION

In this passage, Paul was speaking to the Ephesians about spiritual gifts as related to leadership. The Holy Spirit gives us all, as believers in Christ, gifts of our own. Just as the Ephesian church was to use their gifts to build up the body of Christ and to create unity, so are we.

1. What gift do you have? Are you using your gift(s) to serve the church? If not, why?

2. If you are using your gifts, is your motivation for the "building up" of the church and the glory of God? Explain.

3. How do we make sure we are protected from becoming "children, tossed to and fro by the waves and carried about by every wind of doctrine" (v. 14 ESV)?

4. How have you allowed divisions in your family, community group, circle of friends, Bible study, local church, neighborhood, or workplace to creep into your attitude despite the fact that we are all one body? How will you repent of these practically?

5. We are called "in one hope" and we have "one Lord" (vv. 4–5). What other people or things have you put your hope in? What rules you?

6. Great grace has been extended to you. When is it hard for you to extend grace to others? Why?

7. What is harder for you: speaking the truth, or doing it in a loving way? How will you seek to grow where you are weakest? Are you content with the gifts God has given you? Why or why not? How does your contentment (or lack of it) influence how you use (or don't use) your gifts?

FURTHER STUDY

Review the prior lessons on Ephesians 1–3, and reflect on what you've learned in this study so far. How do you see the first half of the letter informing this section?

Read chapter 10 in *Who Do You Think You Are?*[3] to learn more about spiritual gifts and how God has gifted you.

WEEK 11

READ EPHESIANS 4:17–24.

God reveals his holiness in surprising ways, and a radio interview with the princess of Norway is worthy of mention as an illustration. At the time of the interview, most Norwegian royalty seemed to be caught up in some kind of scandal or other, but the princess lived her life differently. The radio interviewer asked her, "Why do you live differently than the other royals we see? You have such a good reputation by the way you live your life." Her answer was sweet and memorable as she said, "I am the daughter of the king, the way I live represents him and Norway, and I live differently because I want to honor him and my country." Here was a woman living differently because of her identity as the daughter of the king of Norway.

As believers, we also are daughters of the King of kings and Lord of lords. How much more should our identity as daughters of God also reflect and represent Jesus and his church? Therefore, we are called to live in a manner of holiness, not so you or I can look better, but because he chose us to be his daughters. We're given new lives to reflect his image.

OBSERVATION

Paul used the language of walking in Ephesians 4:17 and compared the drastic difference between life in Christ and the life of hardened unbelief. Thankfully, God doesn't leave us to our own efforts. No, the Christian call to holiness is empowered by the same power that caused Jesus to rise from dead!

How did Paul describe the people of the world in Ephesians 4:17?

What had happened to the nonbelievers' thinking (mind, emotions, and will) in verse 18? Explain why.

What is the result of living apart from Christ as seen in verse 19?

How are we to walk? (Hint: read Colossians 1:10 and Philippians 3:17–18.)

What was Paul reminding the readers of in Ephesians 4:20?

What did Paul encourage the Christian to do in verses 22–24?

How is it possible for us to put off our old self and put on the new self? (Hint: see Romans 6:2–6 and Colossians 3:10).

INTERPRETATION:

This portion of Ephesians has set the stage for the rest of the letter and spells out how the Christian's mind is renewed. It also shows a progression from the negative life of unbelievers to the positive life of the Christian.

1. The phrase "learned Christ" that we see in Ephesians 4:20 doesn't appear anywhere else in the Greek Bible. In this context, Jesus is the very content of the teaching. We don't simply learn about Jesus; we get to know the living person of Jesus as he reveals himself to us.

2. What does it mean that we have "learned Christ"? (Hint: see Matthew 11:29.)

3. How can we lay aside the old self?

4. What is the new self that Paul was encouraging his readers to put on?

5. In verses 22–23, what did Paul encourage the church to do as believers? Why?

APPLICATION:

Being created in the likeness of Christ changes the way we see the world, and our desires and actions begin to change. Being a Christian isn't always easy, and it's hard work to say no to sin, but it is our privilege as his redeemed people. Before you knew Christ you didn't struggle with sin, you just . . . sinned. Part of living the Christian life is to having the mind renewed by reading God's Word. Leon Morris, in his book *Expository Reflections on the Letter to the Ephesians,* stated, "There is far more to being a Christian than intellectual achievement, but we should be clear that being a follower of Christ means using the brains God has given us to their fullest capacity."[4]

1. Why is reading scripture important in renewing your mind? Read Romans 12:2.

2. What are you grateful for in your life because of what Christ has done? Take this time to write down the blessings in your life.

3. We all are tempted with former ways of life at one time or another. How do you currently struggle with temptation? Share this with your group.

4. Having a new self changes the way we approach relationships, friends, spouses, children, and the church body. Was there a time this week that you responded sinfully to someone because of your own desires? Take a few minutes now and ask the Holy Spirit to reveal to you if there is anyone that you need to go to and ask for forgiveness.

WEEK 12

READ EPHESIANS 4:25–32.

When was the last time you can recall getting hurt by someone, or getting mad at a situation that was out of your control? As a Christian, your decision to remain angry or to forgive will have a positive or negative impact on the body of Christ, as well as your relationship with Jesus. By God's grace, Christians have the power to make godly decisions through the power of the Holy Spirit.

OBSERVATION:

In Ephesians 4:25–32, the apostle Paul was teaching believers how to live a godly life for the overall edification of the church. While the Ephesians once walked in the passions of their own flesh and were under wrath, they had been given grace and were made alive with Christ through the Spirit. Therefore, they were called to put on and walk in their new self, which is in true righteousness and holiness (v. 24).

1. Paul started verse 25 with the word "therefore," leading us to think about his previous words. Read Ephesians 4:20–24. How do these verses help you understand why Paul was emphasizing the principles found in verses 25–32? What characteristics must be present in order to accomplish the commands in these verses?

2. Why do you think Paul commanded verses 22–24 before verses 25–32?

3. Which characteristics reflect our old nature as children of wrath? Which reflect our new nature in Christ?

INTERPRETATION

The principles Paul was commanding the believers of Ephesus to live out in their daily lives consisted of speaking the truth, edifying others with their words, being angry without sinning, laboring honestly, not grieving the Holy Spirit, and moving from malice to forgiveness. These commands taught them how to live in accordance with the will of God. They were called to be worthy of the family name, and to live in unity in order to build up the body of Christ.

1. Paul began his list of exhortations in verse 25 by stating that falsehood is a part of the old self. Each of Paul's exhortations has to do with personal relationships, and they are intended to foster unity within the body of Christ.

Look up John 17:22–23 and Ephesians 4:15–16 in your Bible. Why is it so important that we function in unity as one body?

2. In Ephesians 4:26–27 Paul said that anger should not be allowed to fester or continue for long, because the consequence of unresolved anger gives the devil an opportunity to divide the body of Christ.

Read the verses below as you consider your answer to this question: What kind of anger do you think Paul was referring to that is righteous and not considered sin?

Righteous Anger
   Matthew 21:12–13
   Mark 3:4–5

Unrighteous Anger
   James 4:1–3
   James 1:19–20

3. Paul says in Ephesians 4:28 that stealing is motivated by the old self and reveals a sinful heart. Now that the Ephesians were alive in Christ, Paul called them to earn an honest living and to contribute to anyone in need.

Read James 2:15–16 and 1 John 3:17. How do these verses help us understand why believers are to live honestly and labor with their own hands in order to give to those in need?

4. Paul exhorted us in Ephesians 4:29 to use our words to give grace to the body of Christ. He called Christians to choose edifying words, so God's grace can be realized as they build up the church according to the occasion. Paul told the church in Colossians 4:6 to always be gracious in speech, in order to know how to answer people. Do you think this

command has any relationship to the command in Ephesians 4:25? Why or why not? What does it mean to "give grace" when speaking (v. 29 ESV)?

5. In verses 30–32 we see that believers are not to "grieve" the Holy Spirit by participating in unrighteous attitudes and actions, such as bitterness, wrath, and anger. Believers can grieve the Holy Spirit. What does that tell you about Him?

How is Paul's model of forgiveness important to our relationship with others?

APPLICATION

It is only through Christ's grace, forgiveness, and the power of the Holy Spirit that we are able to live out the godly principles found in this week's passage. As God, Jesus, and the Holy Spirit care, love, and respect one another, so we are to be likewise unified as one body of Christ and exemplify this unity to the watching world. With this in mind, please discuss the following questions.

1. What truths about this passage do you struggle with? Why?

2. Have there been times when you have held on to anger? What happened that made you angry? Did you experience righteous or unrighteous anger? What might forgiveness look like in your situation?

3. Do you consider yourself a consumer or a generous giver in the body of Christ? In what area(s) is God calling you to change, so you can be a more generous giver to the body of Christ?

4. What is the Holy Spirit revealing to you about your usual style of communication. Do you like to encourage, or are you quick to criticize? Why?

5. Pray and ask God if you are grieving the Holy Spirit in light of this passage. If so, pray that he will change your heart and fill it with the desire to be kind, tenderhearted, and forgiving.

FOR FURTHER STUDY:

1. Memorize and meditate on any verses from this week's passage that you believe Jesus is using to encourage and/or convict you.

2. Choose and reword a statement or scripture into a prayer of response to Jesus.

3. What does God want you to do in response to what you learned today? In what truth does he want you to rest?

WEEK 13

READ EPHESIANS 5:1–21.

When our first mother, Eve, initially sinned, she *chose* to walk in darkness, hide from God, and separate from her husband. As her daughters, we are prone to follow in her footsteps. We don't want others to know who we really are, so we hide our sin in fear that we'll look bad in the eyes of others. In the workplace, we gloss over mistakes, and at home we get frustrated with the kids. In marriage, we get worn out praying the same prayers for our husbands, but we don't want to consider that our sin is as big an issue as theirs, and we refuse to change until they do. We choose our blindness.

When Eve sinned, she saw the fruit was good for food, attractive to the eyes, and desirable in making her wise. Sexual and covetous sins (as specifically discussed in this chapter) follow the same pattern in our lives: we see a specific person or object, notice it is attractive, begin to desire or long for it, and finally take it as our own. We have a real fight on our hands, and it's time to walk in the light and trust Jesus.

OBSERVATION

1. What active words stand out in Ephesians 5:1–2?

   How did Paul refer to Christians here?

   Who are we supposed to imitate? In what way does this passage say we are to imitate God?

2. Ephesians 4:32 introduces chapter 5 by telling us to walk in love by being "kind to one another, tenderhearted, forgiving one another, even as God in Christ forgave you." The chapter then moves into specific ways to imitate God in love.

   In Ephesians 5:3–14, when referring to sexual immorality, Paul used the Greek word *porneia* to describe all types of sexual sins (vv. 3–5). He told the church that they were at one time darkness (like the worshippers of Artemis), but as Christians what are we now?

In what practical ways did Paul talk about how to walk in the light and be imitators of God?

As you've looked at the culture in Ephesus, why do you think Paul reminded the Ephesians how to walk in the light and adopt holy living?

3. Paul reminded us in verses 15–17 that the days are evil and we need to make wise choices with the time we have here. What is the result of looking carefully at how we walk (v. 15)? How will we understand God's will?

4. What did Paul say to do instead of drunkenness in verses 18–21?

What harm does being drunk cause? What did Paul say will happen when we are filled with the Holy Spirit? Compare these.

INTERPRETATION

1. In verses 1–2: Paul referred to Christians as beloved children (esv), reminding us that we are adopted into God's family because of Christ's death on the cross.

2. Just like Ephesus in verses 3–5, our culture is consumed with sexual sin and coveting. Today, idols are sold to us by marketing designed to elicit envious desire. Even if we are not committing sexual sin, we may be participating in conversation about it that God considers gossip or "crude joking" (v. 4 esv). Paul was asking us to be aware of all aspects of idolatry and sexual sin.

We are constantly bombarded with images and opportunities to covet. Even at the grocery store checkout line, there are images of idolatry on the front of popular magazines. What sin are you tempted by as you wait in the checkout line?

3. In verses 6–14 Paul was encouraging the Ephesians to walk as children of light. If we desire to imitate God, then we must remember that "God is light and in Him is no darkness at all," and "if we say that we have fellowship with Him, and walk in darkness, we lie and do not practice the truth" (1 John 1:5–6).

Is there someone in your life that God is calling you to challenge to walk in the light? Are there areas in your life that have remained hidden in the dark?

4. In Ephesians 5:15–17, Paul mentioned that the days are evil. "Look carefully" means to be cautious and avoid harm (ESV). We must ask God's will and make wise choices by studying his word, praying for wisdom, and seeking godly counsel in community.

Are there areas in your life where you haven't been "looking carefully"? What are they?

5. Verses 18–21 are frequently quoted by those who don't drink wine! Wine was a common drink in Bible times (and still is today), but Paul didn't want that to be an excuse to get drunk.

Rather than overindulging in wine, what did Paul call us to? Why?

APPLICATION

1. Where is your loving Father shining his light on your darkness? After you have seen your sin, are you struggling to see your failures as bigger than God's grace?

2. Think about our current culture and compare the ways we worship sexual immorality and covetousness.

Who else do you find yourself imitating in your life instead of Christ?

3. Coveting is jealousy regarding someone or something that you don't have. What are you coveting? What are you thankful for instead?

4. How can you help someone else see her "unfruitful works of darkness" (v. 11)? Can she do the same for you?

5. How is God glorified when we submit to one another? What prevents you from submitting?

FOR FURTHER STUDY

1. Do a word study of all the times "light" is mentioned in reference to God (e.g., John 8:12).

2. Proverbs 15:21 is one of many examples in Proverbs that compares folly and wisdom or principles for living in light versus darkness. Search through Proverbs for more practical encouragement and wisdom for living.

WEEK 14

READ EPHESIANS 5:22–33.

Have you ever been intently driving down the road, focused on your destination, when another vehicle attempted to merge in front of you? Did you speed up, honk the horn, yell, or make hand gestures to express your frustration? You could argue, "I have the right-of-way; you failed to observe the yield sign!" But, nevertheless, at that moment, a decision must be made. "Do I push forward, removing all gaps, or do I yield?"

In Ephesians 5:22–33, Paul was addressing believers in Christ on the topic of the unique roles of men and women within the marital relationship. Previously in Ephesians, we discussed submission in general terms of how believers are to treat one another—with mutual submission (5:21). Here Paul was specifically focusing on the unique relationship of marriage.

OBSERVATION AND INTERPRETATION

(Since this portion of scripture is so teaching oriented, the observation and interpretations sections have been combined)

1. Role of the Wife (Eph. 5:22–24, 33):

   Paul first addressed the wife and gave clear instruction that she is to submit to her own husband, as to the Lord, in everything. Keep in mind, wives are called to submit to their "own husbands," not men in general. The basis for the wife's submission is the relationship of Jesus Christ and his church. She is to symbolically demonstrate the submission of the church to her head, Jesus Christ.

2. Submission: The word "submission" comes from the Greek word *hupotásso*. It means "to place under" or "to subject or submit one's self unto (another)." It infers a voluntary act, not a forced or demanded action. In addition to the Greek definition, *submission* in this passage implies a "voluntary yielding in love."[5]

Look up the word "yield" in a thesaurus and list two or three synonyms and antonyms for it. Which word best describes your current role/attitude toward your husband?

"Yielding" can be portrayed as bending. As a wife, are you bending or bucking? Is this reflective of your posture before God? Is God calling you to change your posture before him and your husband?

3. Respect: Paul's concluding instruction to the wife was to respect her husband. The word *respect* is defined as "to think very highly or favorably of; to admire."[6] Synonyms include: *appreciate, consider, esteem, regard.* Related words: *applaud, approve, commend, praise.*

Respect starts in our thought life. Describe your thoughts toward your husband. Do you condemn him or commend him? Do your thoughts promote oneness, or are they divisive? How do Romans 12:2 and Philippians 4:8 help you as you consider this?

Read the following passages, and note the key phrases or guiding principles of submission found in them: Ephesians 5:21–22, 24; Colossians 3:18.

4. For Singles: Who has God placed in authority over you? Are you willing to seek godly counsel and place yourself under the authority of your church? If you don't know who you should be accountable to, ask your local pastor or elders in your church. Pray for a humble spirit and consider the example of Jesus. If Jesus needed to submit to his Father, then consider how much more we need to submit to Him. (See Hebrews 13:17).

5. Role of the Husband (Eph. 5:23, 25–29, 33):

In verse 23, Paul explained that the husband is the head of the wife, the leader, just as Christ is the head of the church. Paul further instructed husbands to love their wives and described this type of love in detail giving two vivid analogies: (1) Husbands are to love their wives sacrificially as Christ loved the church and willingly gave himself up for her, his bride; and (2) husbands are to cherish and nourish their wives in the same manner that they would care for their own bodies.

Review this passage and describe Christ's love for his bride, the church, and how he expresses it.

In what specific ways can you show love to your spouse in the way Christ loves?

Paul used the terms "nourishes" and "cherishes" in describing a husband's love for his wife. Do you feel cherished above all others? Have you shared these thoughts with your spouse?

APPLICATION

These instructions are simply stated in this passage, but difficult to carry out and apply—truly impossible without help from the Holy Spirit. Examine the scriptures closely before attempting to act. Don't forget that the previous passages in Ephesians (see 1:13–14 and 5:18) are the bedrock for our ability to carry out these instructions. Believers aren't just forgiven of sin and then sent out with a list of demands to carry out in their own power. No, we are given the Holy Spirit, upon salvation, to act in and through us to accomplish God's plan and purposes. In addition, God continuously fills us with the Holy Spirit to empower us to follow His commands.

As a husband and wife fully yield to Christ, and their hearts are bent on serving one another, complementing each other, they truly become one. Ultimately, this yielding portrays the union of Christ and his bride, the church, to the watching world.

1. Do you struggle to submit to your husband? In what ways?

What excuses are you using to justify lack of submission? Are there circumstances under which submission is not required? Discuss with the group how you might deal with these in a godly way.

2. Fear can be a reason behind the struggle to submit. What are you afraid of? What is holding you back from fully yielding to Christ?

Do you need to bend in order to mend your relationship with your spouse?

3. Pray right now and ask the Holy Spirit to convict you of sin, and then ask God to forgive you and to help you turn from it and yield your marriage to him.

4. If you are in an abusive situation, please don't remain silent. Talk to a leader in your church and get the help you need.[7]

WEEK 15

READ EPHESIANS 6:1–9.

Have you ever taken a picture that didn't turn out because the focal point was out of focus? In photography there is a concept called *depth of field*, where some objects are focused and sharp, while others are blurry. The subject still has a predominant view while the surrounding objects may be slightly blurred.

In Ephesians, Paul built the story of who believers are in light of what Jesus has done. In response we are asked to submit to one another out of reverence for Christ. In our relationships, Christ is the sharp focus, and in him the whole picture makes sense. All we do is unto One, and that is Christ.

OBSERVATION

1. What are the four roles addressed in this passage? Paraphrase the commands given for each of them.

Although fathers are addressed in this command, this pertains to mothers as well. Consider both Ephesians 6:1 and Proverbs 1:8–9, "Hear, my son, your father's instruction, and forsake not your mother's teaching, for they are a graceful garland for your head and pendants for your neck" (ESV).

2. The surrounding scripture has addressed wives, husbands, children, and parents within a household. In this culture, slaves and masters are also addressed.

Rather than being a study on what the Bible says about slavery and its ultimate judgment upon it, this section instructs us in how to live in relationship to one another *as believers in light of the gospel.* The Ephesian church existed in a specific social and legal context that included both slaves and masters. There were believers in both groups, and the gospel affected their relationships. In turn, this passage equips us to consider within our own context what difficult work environments and authorities we find ourselves under.

Read the ESV Study Bible reference notes for a brief background on slaves in this culture. As in 1 Corinthians 7:21, Paul encouraged us to be godly in whatever role we are called to. God sees us with equal value (Gal. 3:28).

What are examples of "earthly masters" (v. 5 ESV)?

3. What name of God is revealed in this passage? What characteristic of him do we also learn?

INTERPRETATION

1. Consider why the phrase "do not provoke your children to anger" is contrasted with the command to "bring them up in the discipline and instruction of the Lord" (v. 4 ESV). Why are these two things opposed? Give an example or scenario.

2. Find the two similar phrases showing how children are asked to obey and then how parents are commanded to discipline and instruct.

Elyse Fitzpatrick states: "Neither the Jews nor the Greeks would naturally have employed training that was 'of the Lord'. This phrase would have been peculiar to them. Paul meant it to be so. Those steeped in the law and those steeped in worldly philosophies would have had to think deeply about the implications of the Good News as they sought to faithfully parent their children—just like we do."[8]

3. Discuss the presence of the phrase "of the Lord" and its significance, particularly for parents. In light of the above quote, how do the gospel's specific messages of salvation, forgiveness, reconciliation, humility, etc., influence how we bring our children up in the discipline and instruction of the Lord?

4. Read Ephesians 6:5–7 addressing God's call for those under "earthly masters" (ESV). What characteristics describe an obedient heart?

Consider how this passage continually turns the focus of obedience from the master (or boss) to our greater authority, Jesus Christ. Read Romans 6:22, which calls believers "slaves of God." What is the "fruit" of this slavery?

5. Look over Ephesians 6:5–9 and consider why the passage includes God's character, as it relates to both the slave and to the earthly master.

This common calling of Christians operates irrespective of the social roles you fill. It establishes a core attitude of mutuality that threads through every single relationship. We are one with each other and we are equals, leveled before God, whether apostle or new-hatched convert, tycoon or welfare recipient, genius or retarded, four-star general or buck private, CEO or janitor, competent adult or helpless infant."[9]

APPLICATION

1. Have you sinned in provoking your child to anger? Do you confess to your child your sin of being too harsh? What do you think would happen if you did?

God the Father's specific commands to parents indicate that he knows our weaknesses and tendencies. He leads us to parent well by first bringing us up and instructing us.

2. Please review Ephesians 2:1–7. Jesus came for us when we were "children of wrath." The gospel is a picture of Jesus' pursuit of us in our defiance of him. How does his pursuit encourage you, especially on very difficult days?

3. Where do you struggle to obey with respect and fear . . . with sincerity of heart . . . with serving wholeheartedly? Do you truly believe you are serving Christ as you fulfill your earthly obligations?

4. We will study Ephesians 6:10 in the next session, but notice the use of "in the Lord" again.

Tie together the instructions to family relationships in Ephesians 5:22–6:9, ending ultimately with 6:10 with this last "in the Lord" instruction. Why is it a significant connection for you today? Isn't God a good Father to lead us to a final focus on these words?

5. If you are willing, please pray the following prayer silently, slowly, and with a sincere heart. "Lord, please help us to set our focus intentionally

on you in our household and jobs. Let the full picture be about seeing *you, Jesus,* as we serve and love those in our given roles. Enable us to follow your example in laying our lives down, rendering service in all of our relationships with goodwill as to the Lord and not to man. In Jesus' name, amen."

WEEK 16

READ EPHESIANS 6:10–24.

God, thank you that we are strengthened by your might. We pray that we won't abandon the armor you have provided for our battle. Thank you that Jesus has won the war, and please continue to strengthen us as we face a battle every day.

Paul concluded his letter to the church at Ephesus with a final exhortation. The Christian life is rich in blessings, but not always peaceful and problem free. Believers face a cosmic battle with the forces of darkness, and though the ultimate war has been won, and Jesus is the victor, the battle still wages. We are soldiers for the gospel under attack. Therefore, we must take on the whole armor of God.

OBSERVATION

1. What is the big idea of this passage? How would you title it in your own words?

2. Who is mentioned in this passage?

3. What was Paul's intent in this passage?

4. Why did Paul end Ephesians this way?

INTERPRETATION

1. Read Ephesians 6:10 in the English Standard Version, and mark every use of the word *strength* and its derivatives. How did Paul define our strength? Where does it come from?

2. Ephesians 6:10 exhorts us not to act strong but to *be* strong in the Lord. This strength doesn't come from what we do or say, or from our own resolve; rather, strength comes from the Lord.

The ESV reads "Finally, be strong in the Lord and in the strength of his might," while the NIV reads "Finally, be strong in the Lord and in his mighty power." To distill this verse down to its essence, we are to be strong in the strength of *God's* strength. The Holman Christian Standard Bible best captures the passive tense of the original Greek by saying, "Finally, be strengthened by the Lord and his vast strength." Human strength always fails in the end. Fortunately, we're not required to muscle up and power through our battles. We merely take God at his word that he is strong *for* us.

The theme of strength weaves through the Ephesians epistle. Read Ephesians 1:19–20; 3:16. What else does Paul reveal about our power, might, and strength? What is its source?

Plainly stated, we face a real enemy—the devil schemes to defeat us with rulers, authorities, and cosmic powers of darkness and evil (v. 12 ESV). Just the thought of trying to defend ourselves against such an onslaught could result in never leaving the covers in the morning. But God does not abandon us. Exodus 14 describes a time when the Israelites faced an adversary, Pharaoh. God spoke through Moses and told the Israelites to stand firm. Ultimately, their enemies were defeated by God's sovereign power.

3. Read Ephesians 6:11–14, marking the verbs "put on," "take up," and "stand." What do you learn about the manner in which we engage in battle with the enemy?

4. Paul mentioned the armor worn by Roman soldiers, and the Ephesians would have been familiar with seeing soldiers in uniform. While it's interesting to consider why the analogy of a shield is paired with faith, or righteousness with a breastplate, to get sidetracked with why questions regarding the imagery would be to miss the point. God is our strength, and he called us to take up the protection he has provided in the heat of spiritual battle.

Next to each piece of armor, label whether its function is defensive or offensive.

The final piece of armor Paul mentioned is the sword of the Spirit. It is the only weapon described. What is the sword of the Spirit?

5. Jesus had scripture memorized and ready when temptations arose. Likewise, deep knowledge of Scripture is so important to our daily existence as well. When we memorize God's Word, we are ready to wield it

in moments of temptation and attack. Scripture memory isn't a mental contest, accomplishment, or achievement; it's necessary for enduring in battle until our final day.

Read Matthew 4:1–11. How did Jesus combat the enemy Satan? Record his words in response to Satan's temptation.

6. So far we could outline this passage "Be strong in the Lord, Stand Firm, Put on God's armor." Now read Ephesians 6:18–20. What was Paul's final exhortation? Refer to Matthew 26:41, where Jesus gave the same exhortation to the disciples at Gethsemane.

That's it, friends. Christians are called to fight and defend themselves with God's armor against spiritual attacks, as we go forth spreading the gospel. In battle, we need to put on God's armor, to know and wield God's Word, and to watch and pray. We are victorious in Christ! Our sword cuts to the bone (Heb. 4:12) and brings light to the darkness (Ps. 119:105). And our prayers are powerful and effective (James 5:16). We are more than conquerors in Christ! (Rom. 8:37).

APPLICATION

1. Are you strong in the Lord's strength or your own? What do you need to relinquish control of to be strengthened in the Lord? Practically speaking, how does that change take place?

2. Have you ever experienced a "when you have done all, stand" situation (see Ephesians 6:13)? Please share your testimony of truth that God defends us from the enemy when we put on the whole armor and stand.

3. It is important to note that this passage was addressed to a church body, not just an individual Christian. It's important that we do battle alongside other believers. Do you have Christian community you can count on in battle? How can you support the community of believers where you have been placed? What does it look like for you to battle alongside (not against) other believers?

4. Methodically journal through the different pieces of God's armor. Are there pieces you aren't using although God has made them available? Why not?

5. Who or what are you presently watching and praying over?

NOTES

1. Steve Brown, *Reformed Theological Seminary's Reformed Quarterly*, Fall 2007.

2. John Piper sermon "Far More Than You Think," September 29, 1985, http://www.desiringgod.org/resource-library/sermons/far-more-than-you-think.

3. Mark Driscoll, *Who Do You Think You Are?* (Nashville: Thomas Nelson, 2012).

4. Leon Morris, *Expository Reflections on the Letter to the Ephesians* (n.p.: Baker Publishing Group, 1999), 135.

5. *The Bauer-Arndt-Gingrich-Danker Greek-English Lexicon* (Chicago and London: The University of Chicago Press, 2000), 848, section 1bb.

6. Merriam-Webster's Collegiate Thesaurus, 2nd ed. (2010).

7. If you believe a crime is being committed, call the police. Most states have descriptions online of what counts as domestic violence. Simply search online, for example: "domestic violence Washington state."

8. Elyse Fitzpatrick and Jessica Thompson, *Give Them Grace: Dazzling Your Kids with the Love of Jesus* (n.p.: Crossway, 2011), 84.

9. David Powlison, *Journal of Biblical Counseling* 17, no. 2 (Winter 1999).

STUDENT
MINISTRY
STUDY

STUDENT MINISTRY STUDY

HOW TO USE THE
STUDENT MINISTRY STUDY

Who do you think you are? This is one of the most important questions you will ever be asked. The answer to this question is so crucial that it will determine the way you live your life.

The student material has been designed for students and student leaders to help uncover common misunderstandings about the answer to this question, while leading you and your group to discover who you are in Christ.

Students, this participant guide is for you. Use it to take notes and jot down your answers to the questions as you go through the material.

Student leaders can download the *Leader's Guide* for free at PastorMark. tv. The *Leader's Guide* is designed to help assist you in teaching this material to your student group.

Scripture Reading: Read the assigned passage before you meet with your student group. The passages go along with the topic, and reading them ahead of time will help you prepare for the lesson and the discussion afterwards.

Introduction: The introductions will help you better understand the following Bible lesson. We encourage you to read these in advance to prepare you for your time with your student group.

Breakout Questions: The breakout questions will help you dig deeper into the lessons. To get this most out of this time, we encourage you to answer the questions honestly. Pray and think about them. Taking your time with these questions will help you best understand yourself and discover who you are in Christ.

WEEK 1
I AM _____?

Scripture: Genesis 1:26–27

Who are you? What defines you? Who do you think you are?

These are simple, but extremely important questions. Your answers to these questions affect every part of your life. So, how you answer them will make all the difference in the world.

Take some time to think about it. Who do you think you are?

Are you thinking about what you own, or what you will be someday?

Maybe you're thinking about the sports you play, the musical instruments you've mastered, or how good you are at video games.

Perhaps you're thinking about how many friends you have on Facebook or followers on Twitter.

Maybe this question makes you think about your problems.

Again, who do you think you are?

In the movie *The Bourne Identity*, Jason Bourne was suffering from amnesia and struggled with the answer to this question himself. He knew a lot about himself, but he couldn't answer the most important question of all, "Who am I?" Because he was unsure of his identity, this question drove him like a madman to figure out exactly who he was.

In a lot of ways we're like Jason Bourne. Each of us has an identity crisis, and we're trying to figure out who we really are.

QUESTIONS:

1. Do you relate with Jason Bourne? Do you have a hard time answering the same question, "Who am I?"?

2. Why is it important for us to know who we are?

3. Do you look to what you own, what you do, who you know, what you long to be, and what you've gone through in life in defining your identity?

WEEK 2
I AM IN CHRIST

Scripture: Ephesians 1:1–14

All of us love stories about heroes who have accomplished amazing things. From television shows, movies, and books, everyone loves a great story of courage, sacrifice, and triumph.

This type of story is called a *biography*. In a biography the hero is someone who rescues him- or herself or someone else from a terrible fate. Biographies are always sources of hope and examples of courage, dedication, sacrifice, and triumph.

Biographies are great, but testimonies are even better.

Every Christian has a testimony about Jesus—his life, his accomplishments, and his determination. Testimonies showcase Jesus as the hero who rescues us from sin, death, hell, and the just wrath of God. In Christ, our life is about Jesus and what he has done for us, not about our accomplishments.

We learn a great lesson about biographies and testimonies from the first *Toy Story* movie.

After going through his own personal identity crisis, Buzz Lightyear was crushed and devastated when he finally realized that he wasn't a Space Ranger, but a mere toy. Buzz had lost all hope in his biography.

Seeing Buzz's demise, his friend Woody tells him how much better it is to be a toy than a Space Ranger. Woody offered the hope of a testimony. To encourage Buzz, he said, "Look, over in that house is a kid who thinks you are the greatest, and it's not because you're a Space Ranger, pal. It's because you're a toy. You are his toy."[1]

Who we are and to whom we belong is something all of us need to hear.

God's love for us is not based on our looks, what we wear, what we accomplish, or the even the good works we do. God loves us because we are his child in Christ.

QUESTIONS:

1. What is the difference between a biography and testimony?

2. Read through Ephesians 1:1–14 and find every occurrence of "in Christ" or its variation, like "in Him" or "in the Beloved."

3. After a few minutes ask, "What did you learn about your identity in Christ from these verses?"

4. Did the conversation between Woody and Buzz help you better understand the difference between a biography and testimony?

WEEK 3
I AM A SAINT

Scripture: Ephesians 1:1–2

Johnny Cash is a legend in the music world. He's considered one of the most influential musicians of the twentieth century and was not only inducted into the Country Music Hall of Fame, but the Rock and Roll Hall of Fame and the Gospel Music Hall of Fame. Johnny Cash has some serious cred.

Even though he was a huge success, Johnny Cash wrecked his first marriage and even struggled at points with drugs and alcohol. In spite of his sins, Johnny Cash was a saint.

For Johnny Cash to be considered a saint will raise some questions.

Isn't a saint a morally good person? Someone who does a lot of good things and never causes any trouble? To some, saints are people who appear in paintings, with halos around their heads, or images of Mother Teresa come to mind.

But this isn't the biblical picture of saints at all.

Saints are average, ordinary, everyday-type Christians, with all of their faults and flaws, just like you and me.

You don't need to feed and clothe millions of people, or perform a lot of good works to be a saint. To become a saint requires just one, simple step: be in Christ.

Johnny Cash was a saint, and so are you, if you are in Christ.

QUESTIONS:

1. Is it hard for you to think of someone like Johnny Cash as a saint? Why or why not?

2. To whom did Paul write the letter of Ephesians? *(To the saints who are in Ephesus)*

3. What do you think it means to be a saint? *(Biblically, to be a saint is not based on the good work you do, but the work that Jesus has done for you in living, dying, and rising from death.)*

4. If you have placed your faith in Jesus Christ for the forgiveness of your sins, then he considers you a saint. How does this change the way you think about yourself and live for Jesus?

WEEK 4
I AM BLESSED

Scripture: Ephesians 1:3–14

Sometimes we treat God like a back scratcher. You now, "You scratch my back; I'll scratch yours."

Everyone's made back-scratcher prayers to God before. A back-scratcher prayer is the kind of prayer where you promise God that if he gets you out of a bad situation, you will do something in return. Or, it's the type of prayer when you ask God if he will do something for you if you do something for him.

This is how God gets treated like a back scratcher. "If I do this, will you do that?"

If we're honest, most people have a trading-favors-with-God kind of belief. But did you know this is not taught in the Bible?

Saying this isn't the same as talking about cause-effect decisions, like, if you touch something hot, you'll get burned, or if you cheat on a test and get caught, you will fail.

The Bible isn't about people doing bad things and getting bad things in return. This isn't Christianity at all. This is something more like Karma, and Karma isn't a Christian idea.

Regardless of how amazing a person you are, you cannot manipulate God by being good. You can never do enough good for God to bless you. Attempting to manipulate God into blessing you is as unnecessary as trying to make water wet.

If you're a Christian, nothing else is necessary for you to do to be blessed. You are already blessed in Christ.

QUESTIONS:

1. Do you believe that if you do good or bad things, at some point in time you will get good or bad things in return?

2. Did you know that Jesus took all of your sin debt, and paid the penalty for it? Read Colossians 2:13–14.

3. How does Jesus' death on the cross change your opinion about Karma, and about God himself? *(In spite of our sin, God's love and mercy in Christ covers the penalty that we deserve.)*

4. Read Ephesians 1:6, 12, 14. What is the purpose of God's blessings?

5. How does this change the way you consider the purpose of your life? What does it look like for you to live for God's glory and to enjoy him?

WEEK 5
I AM APPRECIATED

Scripture: Ephesians 1:15–23

In our media-saturated culture, we hear hundreds, if not thousands, of messages every day.

From home, television, school, peers, sports, the Internet, social media, music, movies, and advertisements, we are constantly being bombarded with messages. But isn't it strange that nobody seems to have anything good to say?

If you're paying attention, most of the messages highlight what you *don't* have. You're not working hard enough, your body is flabby, you're not popular on Facebook, you can do better at sports, or you need to buy certain clothes and gadgets to be happy. And we buy into these messages because all of us want to be appreciated by others.

The funny thing about appreciation is that everyone wants it, but no one can ever seem to get it. But what if we stopped fighting for people to appreciate us and instead rested in the love of Jesus?

What others say about you does not determine who you are. As hard as it may be to understand and accept this, your personal value and worth are not based on the opinions of others or on what you own, but on who you are in Christ.

Rest in the knowledge that you are loved and accepted by God in Christ.

QUESTIONS:

1. Do others' opinions determine how you feel or think about yourself?

2. When seeing a new advertisement for an album, phone, or pair of tennis shoes, how does it make you feel? Do you have an overwhelming desire to buy it? Do you feel incomplete without it?

3. Paul celebrated what God was doing in someone else's life. Do you celebrate the success of others?

4. Is there anyone in your life who appreciates you the way Paul appreciated the church in Ephesus?

5. By God's grace, commit to being an appreciative person. Identify up to three ways you can appreciate others.

WEEK 6
I AM SAVED

Scripture: Ephesians 2:1–10

Imagine that you're on a boat at sea.

Your family and friends are with you, and you're having the time of your life. There's fishing, swimming, games, food, and plenty of sunshine. You couldn't think of a better place to be.

As the day progresses, you begin to notice a huge storm forming on the horizon, and you decide to set course for home.

While you're heading for the shore, massive amounts of rain begin pouring down, and the wind blows so hard you think that you're going to get knocked overboard as the huge waves crash against the boat, rocking it from side to side.

You're worried, and rightfully so.

The storm begins to grow in intensity, and before you know it, the boat is tipped over by a ginormous wave.

In an instant, you're submerged in the water and in a state of shock. Thoughts flood your mind. *What just happened? How am I going to survive?*

You're utterly alone, stranded, and unable to save yourself.

After what appears to be an eternity, the storm subsides, and you see the lights of a ship from the coast guard. One of the crew members tosses you a life ring and pulls you in.

This may be a dramatic picture, but it's similar to every person's situation before they meet Jesus. Apart from faith in Christ, we are dead in the water. We are spiritually dead and separated from God, unable to save ourselves. Just as when we're hopelessly stranded at sea, we can't do anything to save ourselves from our spiritual condition.

Thankfully, Jesus can.

In Christ we're saved from our sins and the consequence of death, and made alive to God and reunited with him.

BREAKOUT QUESTIONS:

1. After imagining being stranded at sea, unable to save yourself and dependent upon someone else to save you, do you better understand your need for Jesus?

2. How did Paul describe people? *(Apart from Christ mankind is dead in their trespasses and sins; they follow the course of this world, follow Satan; live in the passions of their flesh, carry out the desires of the body and mind, and are by nature children of wrath.)*

3. What were we saved from? *(From Ephesians 2:1–3 we see that we were saved from the wrath of God.)*

4. What did God do for us "with Christ"? *(God made us alive together with Jesus Christ).*

5. All of us are spiritual dead men and women before God. We're unable to move toward God unless God moves toward us. We are dependent upon his grace and mercy in revealing Jesus Christ to us. How does this change the way you relate and share the gospel with non-Christians?

WEEK 7
I AM RECONCILED

Scripture: Ephesians 2:11–16

Preppies. Punks. Jocks. Geeks. These are just some of the cliques with whom we identify or in which place others.

Cliques are groups we look to for friendship, comfort, and popularity. We believe that if we gain the acceptance of a particular group, then life will be perfect. However, the problem with cliques is they're made up of imperfect people. This means they won't meet your needs and will end up letting you down.

Another thing about cliques is, once you're in one, all other outsiders are black listed or ignored, and sometimes, hated.

Take a moment and think about this. What groups of kids come to mind at your school, in your community, or in your sports league that you make fun of?

Why?

You probably have countless reasons why, but you think less of them for basically one reason: they're not like you or your group.

In Christ all of this changes.

In heaven, the false hope of cliques will be destroyed. Everyone will be unified in Christ. While we can't live this out perfectly today, we should do our best to live in unity with those who are in Christ, no matter whether they're like us or not.

BREAKOUT QUESTIONS:

1. Are you a part of a clique? How do you treat those who are not part of your group?

2. What do you look for with the group of people you hang out with? Fun? Popularity? Friendship?

3. In Christ you are at peace with God. His judgment and wrath no longer stand against you. How does this change the way you approach him?

4. In Christ the invisible walls that separate you from others have been destroyed. How does your faith in Christ change the way you interact with other people?

5. How would you consider your relationships with people in groups different from your own? Is there anything you need to change or repent of?

WEEK 8
I AM AFFLICTED

Scripture: Ephesians 3:1–13

The Christian life isn't easy.

Following Jesus doesn't guarantee that life will be smooth sailing. In fact, Jesus guarantees us that we will experience some level of suffering in our lives by simply being identified with him (John 15:18–21).

Think about it this way.

Have you ever been teased, made fun of, yelled at, pushed around, or even physically harmed for being a Christian? Has anyone ever given you a hard time because you're choosing to honor Jesus by remaining a virgin until you're married?

If you haven't had this experience, take a moment to read the headlines about the 2012 Olympics hurdler, Lolo Jones.

After finishing fourth in the 100-meter hurdle finals in the 2012 games and not winning a medal, Lolo received unprecedented bullying from the media and social networks for. But the attacks against her had nothing to do with her athleticism or performance, but rather with her virginity. The criticism was ridiculous. People argued that if Lolo had had sex, she would have been able to run faster.

You see, Lolo is a devout Christian and has chosen to honor Jesus by remaining a virgin until marriage.

Even though she has suffered under the public eye, this time has given her the opportunity to point to Jesus.

There are countless ways you'll experience some level of ridicule in your life as a Christian. Don't be surprised and don't use these times to fight back. Instead, use these times as an opportunity to brag about Jesus Christ.

BREAKOUT QUESTIONS:

1. Have you ever experienced any negative reactions from others because you identified yourself as a Christian? How did you respond?

2. How do the times when we are mistreated because of our faith in Jesus give us an opportunity to share about him?

3. Read John 15:18–21. Did the world love or hate Jesus? Should we expect the world, in particular non-Christians, to love our beliefs and us?

4. Does knowing that you should expect some level of suffering as a Christian make you reconsider your trust in Jesus? Why or why not?

WEEK 9
I AM HEARD

Scripture: Ephesians 3:14–21

Imagine you're at school, stuck with a personal problem.

You can't find your friends, and for some reason, your parents aren't answering your calls. You're so bothered by your problem that you need to get help right away.

After you think about it, you realize there are only two people available who can help. So, you have to choose between a nice, approachable teacher and a stern one. One teacher knows and cares about you, and the other always seems irritated by your very presence. Who would you choose in this situation?

Unless you like cranky people, you'd choose the nice teacher, who knew you and cared about your situation.

Now, how do you view God? Do you see him as a stern, mean old man who's annoyed with you? Or, do you picture God as he really is: gracious, merciful, and loving?

Your understanding of God will influence your prayer life. If you think he's mean and stern, then you're unlikely to approach him. If you see him as he really is, then you'll be encouraged to talk with him about anything and everything.

God is loving and kind, so why would you not want to go to him?

BREAKOUT QUESTIONS:

1. Do you think God is a mean old man or a loving Father?

2. God the Father is loving and kind. Do you have a hard time accepting this? Why or why not?

3. Read Matthew 6:9. How did Jesus teach his followers to pray?

4. Seeing that God is your Father in Christ, how does this change your prayer life?

WEEK 10
I AM GIFTED

Scripture: Ephesians 4:1–16

There's an old cliché: "There's no *I* in team." Even though there's an *I* in win, a winning team is made up of a group of individuals who play together as a whole.

It's just a fact that some people are more gifted and talented than others. Unless you're a gold medalist, some athletes are faster, stronger, and better performers. Regardless of how good one player is, a single person doesn't win a game. In team sports it's not about the individuals, but about the individuals playing together as a team.

Teams succeed based on the involvement of every player. As an example, if a player doesn't perform well, then the team will suffer and potentially lose the game. Conversely, if players on a team perform well, then the entire team benefits, and they have a better shot at winning.

In a way, team sports give us a picture of the church.

In Christ, you are gifted to serve Jesus and the church. You have been chosen to be a part of the church and involved with the work he's doing. By God's grace, glorify him by using the gifts and talents you have in service in and through the church

BREAKOUT QUESTIONS:

1. Have you played on a team before? What was your experience like? Did one person try to do everything, or did everyone play together as a team?

2. In Christ, you have been gifted and invited by Jesus to help build his church. How does this change the way you think about your involvement with the church?

3. Read 1 Peter 4:10. Why are you given spiritual gifts?

WEEK 11
I AM NEW

Scripture: Ephesians 4:17–24

How is a sports team identified?

Simple. By their uniforms.

Teams have uniforms with symbols and a color scheme. Their uniforms are a way for them to identify each other, represent their school or community, and differentiate them from their opponent.

Could you imagine how confusing it would be if players on a team were allowed to wear whatever they wished during a game? Someone is wearing black. Another person is wearing green. Not only are your teammates wearing different colors; they're even wearing the same colors as the other team.

Yes, you may know who is or isn't on your team. But when things are moving fast on the field, how would you know at a glance who your team members were?

Needless to say, without uniforms things would be confusing during a game.

Christianity teaches us that there are two teams in life and that we play either for one or the other. According to the Bible, one team has Adam as its coach, while the other team has Jesus as its coach.

Apart from faith in Jesus Christ, we are identified with Adam. If you are a player on Adam's team, then you share in his sin and defeat. This is the uniform you wear if you're on his team.

If you are in Christ, then you are considered a part of his team. Being in Christ means that you share in his perfection and victory. This is the uniform you wear on his team, so why would you want to cause confusion by being identified otherwise?

STUDENT MINISTRY STUDY

BREAKOUT QUESTIONS:

1. Who would you say is the coach of your life? Adam or Jesus?

2. The Bible paints a dark picture about our life apart from faith in Jesus. Read Ephesians 4:17–19. How does the Bible describe your life apart from Jesus?

3. Thankfully, in Christ we are transformed into new creations. How does Ephesians 4:24 describe our new life in Christ?

4. Ephesians 4:24 says that our new identity in Christ is to be put on like clothing. How do we put on this new clothing?

WEEK 12
I AM FORGIVEN

Scripture: Ephesians 4:25–32

Who are you angry with right now?

Think about it for a moment. Maybe it's a friend who lied behind your back. Maybe a teacher gave you an unfair grade on an assignment you worked really hard on. Maybe it's something even worse that you don't even feel you can talk about.

Whatever it is, if you've been wronged, you're right to be angry.

But remember, you're not the only person who has ever been offended. God has been offended too.

God created the world to be a place of *shalom*. Have you ever heard that word before? *Shalom* is a word the Hebrew Bible uses as a way to describe peace, justice, and flourishing. When we sin against God and others, we are vandalizing shalom, and God is right to be angry with us.

And guess what? God has caught each of us red-handed, spray paint in hand, vandalizing his world. All of us have lied, harmed others and disrupted in some way what God has intended to be good.

We're all vandals of God's shalom.

But I have some good news. If you are in Christ, God doesn't hold your sin against you. Forgiveness is never easy, and it may take time. But once you recognize the depth of your own sin against God, you will want to show compassion with others who have sinned against you.

Forgive as God in Christ forgives you.

BREAKOUT QUESTIONS:

1. Think about one time you were wronged or offended by someone else. How did you respond?

2. Read Ephesians 4:32. How do receive forgiveness from God?

3. Read Ephesians 4:32 again. How does Jesus want us to be toward other people, and why?

4. Is there anyone who you've sinned against from which you need to ask forgiveness?

WEEK 13
I AM ADOPTED

Scripture: Ephesians 5:1–21

There are many similarities between the gospel and adoption.

For instance, before a family adopts a child, that child is not considered a part of his or her family. It's the same way with us and God's family.

Apart from faith in Christ, we are not a part of God's family. We are actually considered "children of disobedience" (Eph. 2:2 KJV).

Thankfully, our relationship with God changes through faith in Jesus Christ.

In Christ God is your Father, and you are considered his beloved child. Not only are you considered his child; you are considered his "beloved child." Regardless of your relationship with your earthly father, your Father in heaven loves you.

If you're a Christian, God the Father has freely chosen to spiritually adopt, love, live with, and bless you. Think about it. This is huge.

If you don't have a good earthly father, you now have a perfect heavenly Father. And if you did have a good earthly father, you now have the additional blessing of your perfect heavenly Father.

BREAKOUT QUESTIONS:

1. Do you sense that you are a son or daughter of God? Do you have a desire to call him Father?

2. In Christ God is your Father, and you are considered his beloved child. How does this change the way you relate with God?

3. What does Ephesians 5:1 say we are to be? How are we supposed to do this?

4. How does Ephesians 5:3–21 compare children of God to children of disobedience?

5. What is the goal of Jesus Christ for your life?

WEEK 14
I AM LOVED

Scripture: Ephesians 5:22–33

Have you heard of horticulture?

Probably not, but that's okay.

Horticulturists help plants grow through various means and methods. One method is called *grafting*.

When plants are grafted, a stem from one plant is taken and joined to another plant. Sometimes this takes place naturally, and many times people do this to help a struggling plant or to encourage the growth of a good plant.

Grafting is a great picture of a biblical reality.

When we place our faith in Jesus, we are completely changed by him. We are changed so much that we are considered new creations. He not only changes us, but he grows us into the person he desires for us to be.

Like a stem that was taken from one tree and placed on another, we have been removed from a tree of sin and death and grafted and connected to Christ.

But if a clipped stem doesn't get connected to another tree, it will eventually die and wither away because it cannot receive the nourishment it needs. We are like stems, and we need to stay connected with Jesus so we can be nourished and grow.

BREAKOUT QUESTIONS:

1. Have you placed your faith in Jesus Christ? If so, would you say that your life has changed as a result of meeting Jesus?

2. Read Ephesians 5:29. How does Jesus treat the church?

3. How would you consider your relationship with Jesus? Is he someone you go to each and every day for nourishment?

4. Does knowing that Jesus is the one who transforms you into the person he wants you to be change the way you live for him? Why or why not?

WEEK 15
I AM REWARDED

Scripture: Ephesians 6:1–9

Imagine a summertime scene. You're at the beach, walking along the seashore. While you're enjoying the view of the sun setting in the distance, you notice a disturbance in the water. As your eyes focus through the glare, you notice a boy struggling to swim. He's screaming for help, and you see that no lifeguards are on duty.

You dive into the water and bring him safely back to shore. Both of you are exhausted, but thankfully you're safe. The young boy you saved is so grateful. He can't keep from telling you how thankful he is.

Later that evening, you get a knock on your door. When you answer, you see that the boy you saved is there with his family, and they're there to thank you for saving their son. As an expression of their appreciation, his family rewards you with a thousand dollars.

The reward is amazing. You didn't anticipate getting something in return. You simply wanted to help someone who was in trouble.

Some people may struggle with the idea of receiving a reward from God for their faithfulness. But it's not as though we do good in order to receive rewards; each of us does good out of the overflow of a changed heart.

A firefighter who saves a person in danger from a burning building doesn't expect a reward. He's simply honored to do his job. Similarly, because of our identity in Jesus, we're able to gladly serve others as those under the gracious leadership of King Jesus.

BREAKOUT QUESTIONS:

1. In heaven you will receive rewards for your faithfulness. Does the promise of rewards encourage you to live for Jesus today? Why or why not?

2. Read John 17:3. How is eternal life described?

3. Who is in authority over you? Is it a parent, teacher, or employer? How do you treat those in authority over you?

4. Who are you in authority over at work, home, church, or any other place? How would those under your authority say that you treat them?

WEEK 16
I AM VICTORIOUS

Scripture: Ephesians 6:10–24

Have you ever heard someone say that the Christian life is like warfare?

It's true. But there is one important fact about this analogy that some people forget: while we are in a spiritual battle, Jesus has won the victory in the war.

When victory is declared in war, the soldiers celebrate. But that doesn't mean there aren't still battles to face. Although victory has been declared, our enemy is still stirring up pockets of rebellion, and we still have to fight battles in this life.

When it comes to spiritual warfare, there are two errors many Christians can make. They are either so terrified by the ongoing warfare that they're unable to move forward in life, or they don't believe that we have an actual enemy.

The Christian author C. S. Lewis said, "There are two equal and opposite errors into which our race can fall about the devils. One is to disbelieve in their existence. The other is to believe, and to feel an excessive and unhealthy interest in them" (*The Screwtape Letters* [New York: HarperCollins, 2001], ix).

Those unaware of the enemy's schemes don't have a chance in the midst of their spiritual battles. But thankfully, our hero, Jesus Christ, has dealt Satan a fatal blow and defeated him once and for all. Christians take great confidence in that fact, and it prepares them for the battles they face in life, knowing Jesus has secured victory once and for all.

Regardless of the battles you face, rest by faith in the victory Jesus has secured for you.

BREAKOUT DISCUSSIONS:

1. Have you ever thought that being a Christian was supposed to be easy?

2. Read Ephesians 6:10–12. How do these verses describe the spiritual war we're in?

3. The bad things in our lives are often an attack from our enemy, a consequence of sin, or the results of our own bad choices. How does knowing Jesus has defeated your enemy encourage you?

4. Physical weapons do not work in a spiritual battle. With what weapons does Ephesians 6:13–20 say we should fight?

NOTES

1. *Toy Story*, directed by John Lasseter (1995), DVD.

CONCLUSION

James M. Gray (1851–1935), author of *How to Master the English Bible*, described the experience that led him to pray that God would teach him how to master the Word. He met a man whose life evidenced such peace, rest, and joy that he questioned him about how he had come to be this way. The answer? By reading Ephesians—not once, but fifteen times. His friend, speaking of when he had finished his final reading of Paul's letter, went on to say, "I was in possession of Ephesians, or better yet, it was in possession of me, and I had been 'lifted up to sit together in heavenly places in Christ Jesus' in an experimental sense in which that had not been true in me before, and will never cease to be true in me again."[1]

Dear reader, you've just finished sixteen weeks of studying Ephesians. Whether you studied alone or with a group, we're so glad you've journeyed with us. You've been *in* Ephesians, and it is our fervent hope that it is now *in you*. How have you been changed as you studied this book? What has God revealed to you as you've sought him in its pages?

The mere act of reading or studying does not change us. Mastery is the work of the Holy Spirit, who teaches and guides us as we seek him, and who promises that we will find him when we search for him with our whole hearts (Jer. 29:11–13). As you have studied Ephesians, what guidance have you received? What truths have become more real to you? How has repentance come? Have you experienced God's love in a new way? Please share this with someone! As you do so, we pray that you will have boldness to proclaim the gospel of love with faith (Eph. 6:23).

Grace be with you, and "with all who love our Lord Jesus Christ with love incorruptible" (6:24 ESV).

---

1 Quoted in Ann Voskamp's blog *"A Holy Experience"* article titled "The 1 Habit at Every Meal That Will Change Your Life" May 29, 2012 5/29/12.